T0129066

Embrace
the Struggle

ZIG ZIGLAR
AND JULIE ZIGLAR NORMAN

Embrace
the Struggle
Living Life on Life's Terms

HOWARD BOOKS
A DIVISION OF SIMON & SCHUSTER, INC.

NEW YORK NASHVILLE LONDON TORONTO SYDNEY

Published by Howard Books, a division of Simon & Schuster, Inc.
1230 Avenue of the Americas, New York, NY 10020
www.howardpublishing.com

Embrace the Struggle © 2009 Zig Ziglar

Library of Congress Cataloging-in-Publication Data

Embrace the struggle / [compiled by] Zig Ziglar.
    p. cm.
1. Consolation. 2. Suffering—Religious aspects—Christianity. I. Ziglar, Zig.
    BV4905.3.E43 2009
    248.8'6—dc22   2009002911

ISBN   978-1-4767-3903-8

10   9   8   7   6   5   4   3   2   1

Manufactured in the United States of America

For information regarding special discounts for bulk purchases, please contact: Simon & Schuster Special Sales at 1-866-506-1949 or business@simonandschuster.com.

The Simon & Schuster Speakers Bureau can bring authors to your live event. For more information or to book an event contact the Simon & Schuster Speakers Bureau at 866-248-3049 or visit our website at www.simonspeakers.com.

Edited by Denny Boultinghouse
Interior design by Jaime Putorti

To the Redhead,
my bride of sixty-two years,
the only woman I've ever loved,
and the most important person in my life
Sure do love you, sweetheart!
Zig Ziglar

I dedicate this book to my beloved husband, James C.
Norman. He is the most important person in my life. His
sense of humor brings me great joy, but it is his wisdom and
spiritual strength that make me respect, admire, and love
him. I feel safe and secure in his love,
and I treasure every day that is ours.
Julie Ziglar Norman

Contents

Foreword

Zig Ziglar, my father, is in a struggle right now—a struggle so profound and so real that by sharing it with you, I believe you will be filled with hope and encouragement. The gift that God has given Dad is the gift of encouragement and the ability to transfer hope to others so that they can rise above whatever circumstance they are in. As Dad has always said, "Getting knocked down in life is a given. Getting up, starting from where you are and moving forward, is a choice."

On March 7, 2007, our family experienced what Dr. James Dobson calls "a suddenly." I was out of town when I got the call. I went numb as I listened to my sister Cindy's voice. "Dad fell down the stairs. He has a serious head injury." Suddenly, our family joined millions of other families facing similar circumstances, and life became very different. Dad, at eighty years of age, lost the vitality for which he was renowned; he no longer moved with the energy and agility of even a sixty-five-year-old man. Almost overnight he aged fifteen-plus years and, thus, began his struggle to live with and overcome the effects of a brain injury.

The next weeks were anxious ones as we figured out the impact of the accident and the possibilities for recovery. The calendar became filled with doctor's appointments and more doctor's appointments. Life was changing fast. But the amazing thing was that Dad's attitude never changed. I knew that he hurt all over from falling down a sixteen-step staircase onto a marble floor. I could see that his balance was impaired and his short-term memory was "really short," as he likes to say, but still he was as optimistic and, if possible, even more loving than before the fall. As usual, he was more concerned for us than he was for himself.

"Focus on what you can do, not what you can't do." I have heard Dad say that hundreds of times. "It isn't what happens to you, but how you respond to what happens to you that makes the difference." "Go as far as you can see, then you can see farther." These are words my father has taught and words he lives by daily. And that is why I'm so excited about this book. Once again my father is using his circumstances, as unfortunate as they may be, to encourage others in their own struggles. As my sister Julie says, he is willing to be transparent, and he continues to write and speak because he wants to show his audiences that life on life's terms is well worth living. Life may never be the same again, but that doesn't mean it can't be just as wonderful and fulfilling—in an entirely new and different way.

My wish for you as you journey through this book is that you will count your blessings until your gratitude bucket is full, and if you or someone you love is in a struggle, take courage and press on because, as the Ziglar family has learned, it is in the depths of the struggle that God reveals His eternal blessings.

Embrace the struggle,
Tom Ziglar
Proud son of Zig Ziglar

Embrace
the Struggle

Introduction

I'm convinced that in the last year the overwhelming majority of people have been struggling with some kind of concern—personal, family, business, health, relationships—you name it. I know I certainly have! It seems that struggles just happen over the course of time. The question is how do you handle them?

Through the years I've spoken about and written often on how to overcome negative situations, but as a motivational/inspirational speaker and author, I personally have spent the majority of my time focused on how to accomplish the next positive achievemen. In the past I believe I have given an honest and realistic picture of how to address struggles, but as you know, what we know is a result of what we've learned. And the things we learn firsthand have a much greater impact on us and better position us to help others deal with similar circumstances. In fact, the Bible tells us this is so: "Blessed be the God and Father of our Lord Jesus Christ, the Father of mercies and God of all comfort, who comforts us in all our tribulation, that we may be able to comfort those who are in any trouble, with the comfort with which we ourselves are comforted by God" (2 Corinthians 1:3–4 NKJV).

Until now, my greatest life struggle has been dealing with the death of my forty-six-year-old daughter, Suzan. I wrote extensively in *Confessions of a Grieving Christian* about how I grappled with my grief and how God comforted me. Not surprisingly, that book has been the one of mine that has generated the most letters from readers. Why? Because that topic directly addresses an emotional struggle all of us eventually face in our lives. Generally, you don't read a book about grief unless you are grieving. And you typically won't gravitate toward a book on overcoming struggles unless you, or someone you love, are in the midst of a struggle. If you find this to be your case, you my friend are reading the right book!

I know without a doubt that the personal struggle I've been going through since my fall has given me insight that I could not have had otherwise. I've been overwhelmed time and time again as I have discovered that the principles I've taught through the years apply to my present circumstances more completely than they ever have at any other time in my life. And, amazingly, the simplest concepts of all have proven to be the most applicable life buoys for me.

The pages that follow this introduction are full of inspiring stories of individuals who have faced struggles and not only survived but live lives far more fulfilling than they ever experienced before their struggles began. Many of the stories come from individuals who, upon hearing about my brain injury, sought to encourage and comfort me with the comfort that God had extended to them during their struggles.

I will share with you the principles and scriptures that have served as lifelines for me and explain how I have applied them to my struggle. You will hear how my struggle has impacted and influenced the lives of my wife, the Redhead (When I'm talking about her, I call her the Redhead. When I'm talking to her, I call her Sugar Baby. Her name is Jean.), my son, Tom, my daughters, Cindy and Julie, and my granddaughter Katherine. You'll also learn how this has impacted my speaking career, my writing, and the wonderful staff I'm blessed to have at our company, Ziglar, Inc.

My personal struggle is health related, but this book deals with not only struggles that physical limitations create but also financial, spiritual, family, and relationship struggles. This book is about living life on life's terms. It is about knowing what you can change and what you can't change and learning how to live your life with an enthusiastic expectation for what is yet to come. Where there is a struggle, there is life. For that we can be grateful!

1

The Fall and the Future

I get lots of ideas when the lights go out at night and it gets very quiet. Sometimes they come when I first lie down to sleep; other times I wake up with an idea racing through my mind. But regardless of when an idea comes, I have made it a habit to get out of bed and write the idea down before it disappears into my dreams. You should do the same.

I've also made it a habit not to disturb the Redhead if I can possibly help it, and that night was no exception. I quietly slid out of bed and hurried toward my office, which is across the hall and to the right of the head of the staircase. As usual, I did not turn on a light. I had traveled that particular path thousands of times in the twenty-two years we'd lived in our home. However, in all those years I had never accidentally put my left foot down where the second floor ended and the first step down our staircase began! Let's just say that misstep more than disturbed the Redhead!

Most of what I am writing at this point is information my family filled me in on after the accident. Since I was unconscious for several minutes, I have absolutely no recall of what happened after I fell, but from what the Redhead tells me, she grabbed the phone and dialed 911 as soon as she realized I was tumbling down the stairs. An ambulance was dispatched, and help was at the house within a few minutes of my fall.

"The Call"

While the paramedics attended to me, the Redhead called our children. By then it was about 10:30 p.m., so seeing our name come up on caller ID at that hour struck fear into our children's hearts. And this time, I'm sorry to say, their fear was not unfounded. My son, Tom, refers to that night as the night he got "the call." I'm quite sure each of you has had "the call" at one time or another and can relate to what our children were experiencing. I'm grateful that all three of them, including Tom who was out of town, hurried to the hospital to help their "elderly parents"—that is what I call us when I'm about half-teasing and half-relieved that our kids are hovering around us, willing and eager to help.

Over the next several hours it became apparent that my left side took the brunt of my fall. When I landed at the bottom of the stairs, I hit my head on the marble floor and then slammed it against the front door. Please don't ask for a reenactment—you get the picture! I had to spend a few nights at the hospital so the doctors could monitor the two areas where my brain had a bleed, and I needed some time to get used to the positional vertigo that I began to experience about twelve hours after I fell. Amazingly, I suffered no broken bones, but I can testify that I was one sore and dizzy guy!

What we didn't know when I finally left the hospital was how seriously my short-term memory had been affected. Sometimes it is nice to be a little clueless. Everyone in the family has had ample time to adjust to the fact that my short-term memory is very, very, short. Now we are all learning how to live with that fact.

Life *is* change. On March 7, 2007, my life changed completely with one, simple, misplaced step. Some would say it changed for the worse, and by human standards they would be entirely right. Fortunately, and I can assure you this is not by chance, the one verse that I've written in the majority of books I've been asked to autograph, the verse that I believe encourages people most in the midst of their troubles, Romans 8:28, "We know that all things work together for good to them that love God, to them who are the called according to his purpose" (KJV), is the verse that allows me to know that God will use this season of my life, difficult though it may be, for His glory and my ultimate benefit.

By human standards my fall down the stairs and the vertigo and the brain injury that resulted in my short-term memory loss would seem to dictate an end to my long and much-loved career, but I'm here to tell you that, even with its problems, my life is more inspiring, more intriguing, and more fulfilling than ever. For me, when life does take an unexpected turn, it is somewhat like taking a hike on a new trail; I can't wait to see what is around the next bend. If the going gets really rocky, I might start hoping smoother ground is just ahead or that I'm close to the end of the trail where I can take a long desired break from the grueling journey. But my enthusiastic expectation for what is yet to come, for what God has planned for me and my life, never wavers. I trust Him.

I also trust my family. Many years ago I told my family that I was concerned that I might not realize it myself if I started to lose my edge and my speeches were no longer as effective as they should be. I did not want to embarrass myself, so I asked them to promise that they would tell me if they ever thought it was time for me to step down from the stage. As I got older and started experiencing some of what I'd call the usual memory loss that happens when we pass the ages of fifty, sixty, and then seventy, the children often checked on me to be sure I was still able to deliver. Thankfully, they were discreet, and until after the accident I didn't even know they had already begun checking me out periodically. They took their assignment seriously, and I'm glad they did.

It is true that as I neared the age of eighty, I began to rely on notes to help me keep my place as I was speaking. But I figured that most folks rely on notes by the time they are eighty, so I wasn't at all concerned about how my audience would perceive my occasional pass by the podium to reference my outline. My daughter Julie reviewed the DVD of the Get Motivated Seminar engagement I did in San Bernardino, California, on March 6, 2007, the day before my accident, and she assures me that I was still completely stageworthy at that point. Unfortunately, my brain injury had such a profound effect on my short-term memory that the ability to reference an outline was beyond me. I could look at the outline, but I couldn't remember the last point that I had made. To add insult to injury, the vertigo I was experiencing made it virtually impossible for me to even walk around the stage safely.

The Dilemma

Obviously, I had a real dilemma. I book engagements months and years in advance, and there were several engagements pending when I fell. I know companies and individuals alike are negatively impacted if I can't keep an engagement, so I have always done everything in my power to be where I'm expected. I've sometimes missed the funerals of my siblings and friends, and I've spoken when I probably should not have due to illness, but I always felt like my responsibility to show up according to plan was paramount. I can still hear my mother saying, "If a man's word is no good—he is no good." I had given my word.

Situations like the one I was in create circumstances that make a fellow really grateful to have good family relationships. I knew I could count on the help of my family, and I got it in spades! The Redhead, Tom, Cindy, and Julie enlisted the help of my doctors who were working with me after my accident, as well as the help of my friends and associates, to determine if I should find a way to continue speaking or stay home and concentrate on my writing.

My family was open to seeing how I would progress, but they were concerned about the very real possibility that my vertigo might cause another fall and that traveling would put me in more vulnerable positions than staying close to home would. When they discussed the idea that it might be time for me to retire from public speaking, it was quickly followed by a concern that God might not be done with using me on the stage, and none of them wanted to be responsible for suggesting I stop if that was, in fact, the case. However, it was crystal clear that short of an outright miracle I would not be giving the kinds of speeches my audiences had come to expect.

The doctors had said that I might recover more of my short-term memory with time as my brain healed, but they couldn't be sure what the ultimate outcome would be. More than two years have passed since my fall, and it seems that I have good days and other days. (You know there are no bad days. After all, some people didn't wake up today, so compared to them, I'm having a better-than-good day!) Since I am over eighty years of age, we are taking the conservative approach to my medical options. We're taking our time and applying the good old Ben Franklin approach I've taught all these years: divide a page from top to bottom, put positive benefits of procedures/therapies in one column and possible negative outcomes in the other, and we'll let the obvious, as well as prayer, determine our decisions.

I'll go into more detail later about some of the therapies, supplements, exercises, and medical treatments friends and even clients have suggested and that we've tried, but for now I want you to know that we've never stopped looking at possible treatments for what ails me. We pray about the treatments and supplements we are told about, and if we feel God is leading me to try them, I try them. My doctors remain supportive and encouraging about the possibilities the future holds.

My associates, particularly those who also speak on public platforms, were and still are concerned about my retaining my dignity and going out on top. The thought of me—in many cases their mentor—performing differently and faltering here and there before an audience is almost unthinkable. I love them for wanting to help me be remembered as I was before the accident. And I love them for personally helping me move ahead, to do what God puts in front of me to the best of my ability.

The Immediate Solution

Thankfully, the only speaking engagement I had to miss immediately after my fall was for my friends and business associates Peter and Tamara Lowe at one of their big Get Motivated Seminars in Houston, Texas, on March 13, 2007. After a lot of in-depth examination by no less than five doctors, it was determined that I had retained almost all of the information I have taught over my many years as a speaker and author, and that I was totally "present" when being spoken to. The only new memory problem I had was with the most immediate short term. When questioned, I could answer without any hesitation; but if you asked me what you had asked me when I finished answering the question, I could not tell you. Yes, my memory about current events is that short! (You're probably wondering how this book got written, and I'll tell you—we are both the beneficiaries of the good help I have. Between my executive assistant, Laurie Magers, my editor/daughter, Julie Ziglar Norman, and others on my staff, we got it done!)

Since I could recall information when asked, Peter Lowe came up with the idea of changing my speaking format. For years I have been known for my energetic, highly physical speaking style. Some people have even accused me of being more than enthusiastic during presentations. I liked to somewhat live out the stories while I was telling them, and I thought standing stock still behind a podium might block or slow down the words that came flying out of my mouth at the rate of 250 per minute with gusts up to 450. You would naturally assume that it was my vertigo that put an end to all my physical on-stage activity, but it really had more to do with the fact that we couldn't find anyone who felt comfortable chasing me around the stage to ask the next question in our new interview format! Sorry, I couldn't contain myself.

Sitting down for one-on-one interviews on stage came about through a combination of my being unsteady on my feet and my mind's not keeping track of what I'd already said. Peter Lowe interviewed me for the first time in Boise, Idaho, on March 27, 2007, just twenty days after my fall, but after a few engagements it occurred to him that my associates, Bryan Flanagan and Krish Dhanam, both having shared the Get Motivated Seminar platforms with me on many occasions, might be a better fit for the interviewer role. They have both taught my material, and they've studied it in order to apply it to their lives. They can tell most of my stories almost word for word, and in the event I had trouble recalling any answer to their questions, they could help out by prompting me toward the answer or outright supplying the answer if it still eluded me. It made perfect sense to ask them to interview me at the Get Motivated Seminars. Fortunately, they both agreed, and with great faith we pressed forward to keep my commitments.

Love and Honor

Both Krish and Bryan did an excellent job of interviewing me on stage. They carefully laid out their questions so that we could cover several different areas of interest, such as the mental, physical, spiritual, financial, and relational sides of life. Their goal and mine was to continue to give the audience valuable, applicable, life-improving information in an entertaining way.

I cannot express fully the gratitude I have for these two men. Engagement after engagement, they tweaked their questions as they learned better how to deal with my short-term memory. They spent hours and hours working on how to make me look my very best. They learned how to highlight the good and minimize the imperfections that were bound to show with the kind of brain injury I suffered.

We continued on this course with the public seminars, but we had to address what we, as a company, would do about my corporate engagements and about my two-day Born to Win (BTW) seminar that I had hosted since the 1970s. Tom was the president of our company at that time (now he is the CEO), and I sorely wish that all the weight of this problem hadn't fallen squarely on his shoulders, but he handled and continues to handle the business beautifully.

Tom decided that we'd notify the corporations I was scheduled to speak for about my accident and the change to an interview format and let them decide if they wanted to keep their engagements or cancel. He also decided that we would not book any more corporate events for the foreseeable future and that we would promote the upcoming Born to Win seminar as the final one.

The Last Born to Win Seminar

I know rock stars have farewell tours, sometimes every four or five years, but I had never considered that I might actually "plan" to do any of the things I do for the last time. I've always figured I'll die while I'm still doing what I love doing. When folks say they've heard I'm retired, I say with mock surprise, "Retired! Friend, you weren't listening! I said I was reFIRED! I'm not gonna ease up, shut up, let up, or give up until I'm taken up! Matter of fact, I'm just getting warmed up!"

Some people might think that's reaching a little far for a man who has celebrated the sixty-first anniversary of his twenty-first birthday. (For those of you who are mathematically challenged, that means I'm eighty-two years old.) But I am truly the kind of guy who goes after Moby-Dick in a rowboat and takes the tartar sauce with him! Which will help you understand that it was with a bit of trepidation that I agreed to the "last" Born to Win seminar.

It wasn't long before I understood why rock stars have so many farewell tours. They sell out—fast! I was overwhelmed at the immediate response to the announcement. Many who attended Born to Win did so several times through the years. Some brought their employees; others came with their whole families in tow. Larry Carpenter particularly stands out in my mind. He attended forty-five times over twenty-seven consecutive years. His beautiful wife, Lisa, and their three sons participated more times than I can remember. Larry also financially sponsored nearly two hundred people down through the years, because he wanted the people he cares about to experience what he experienced there. The last Born to Win was no exception. He brought his whole family and, as we'd say down home, a passel of friends to boot! That event was like old home week for the Redhead and me. We got to see so many people we'd come to know and love. We were in "tall cotton" the whole time.

Because of my accident, my involvement had been scaled down a great deal, but I was scheduled to have three different interview sessions with Krish Dhanam and a great deal of time mixing and mingling with the participants. Krish did the interview the first evening but later fell ill; another long-time associate and friend, Jill Tibbels, agreed to do the Saturday-morning interview, which went off exceptionally well. Jill always does an incredible job of anything we ask her to do. That's just one of the reasons we're so grateful for her association with us, which spans more than twenty-five years.

Tom came up with the idea of making this final BTW more intimate and special by having a "family" session where the Redhead, Tom, Cindy, and Julie joined me on the stage in a living-room setting to tell stories about what it was like having me for a husband and father. I often tell people that if I'd known how much fun grandkids were going to be, I would have been a whole lot nicer to their parents! I'd like to add that had I known my wife and children would be taking the stage to talk about me . . .

We all had a marvelous time, but I suspect my jaw was dropped open most of the time. I had no idea that I had raised so many hams! All three of my children had the audience holding their sides. Honestly, I didn't know that growing up and working with me had provided them with so much funny material! And when the Redhead chimed in, people were almost rolling on the floor. It was as if my family had been saving up for this one occasion. It was all in good, loving fun, and the ones I love most in this world did get around to saying that they loved *and* respected me, so all's well that ends well.

Another Unexpected Twist

Except, as is often the case, what appears to be an ending is anything but. That afternoon of August 25, 2007, was another beginning for me with my daughter and long-time editor, Julie Ziglar Norman. I love seeing the hand of Providence in my life. Julie became my editor as a result of having won a place at the biannual Writers Workshop that *Guideposts* hosts to develop new talent for their magazine. John and Elizabeth Sherrill—long-time roving editors for *Guideposts* and well-known coauthors of Corrie ten Boom's *The Hiding Place* as well as David Wilkerson's *The Cross and the Switchblade* and Brother Andrew's *God's Smuggler*—noted that Julie was a natural at editing. When Julie told me they, and a few others who were leading the workshop, had commented on her editing ability, I immediately knew I needed her to help me with my books. Sixteen years and twenty-one books later we're still writing away. This book is our first effort as coauthors. With my short-term memory loss, the kind of help I needed was more in-depth than the usual editing Julie has done in the past.

And now we're speaking together as well! Jay Hellwig, my driver and personal assistant at that time and the husband of Jill Hellwig, our number one salesperson for more than fourteen years, noticed that the Born to Win attendees responded enthusiastically to what Julie had to say from the stage. Jay told Tom that he thought it would be a more natural fit to have Julie interview me at the Peter Lowe Get Motivated Seminars. He pointed out that because of our father/

daughter relationship she could more comfortably interrupt me if I started to repeat myself and, after all, she had been editing everything I'd said in print for years; she knew all my material. It was such an obvious fit that I wondered why I hadn't thought of it myself! Julie, it seems, had been preparing all along to help me at this time in my life.

It made sense to Tom, too, and when he asked Julie if she would travel with me and her mother and interview me on stage, she agreed without hesitation.

2

We Can All Relate
to the Struggle

Julie took the stage with me for the first time on September 6, 2007, in Washington, DC. When we were waiting beforehand in the Green Room, she kept mumbling something about the scripture that talks about taking your thoughts captive. She was asked by the seminar organizers if she would like to see the stage and how the audience was positioned so she would know what to expect. She quickly declined, saying there are times when it is better not to know what to expect.

I hadn't given it much thought, but my daughter was about to speak with me in front of eighteen thousand people. Prior to that day she had only spoken once to a group of about three hundred people, and then her sister Cindy was by her side. Between the two of them they spoke for five minutes. Julie knew there were going to be thirty-five long minutes on the clock when we stepped foot on that stage, and she refused to give it a second thought. She says she wasn't scared because she knew she was going out there with her daddy. I believe she wasn't scared because God was enabling her to do what He put in front of her to do, and that was to help me.

What happened after we got up on that stage almost blew me away! Julie had decided to surprise her daddy by doing a pretty good impersonation of how I used to speak. First she made sure I was safely seated and headed for the front of the stage, asking one of my most often used opening questions as she went. Having made the appropriate alterations, she said, "How many of you have either seen Zig Ziglar before, or else this is your first time?" She then thrust her arms up in the air, like I would have, and said, "May I see a show of hands, please?"

As the laughter and applause died down, she walked to the edge of the stage and said, "Well, if you have seen Zig Ziglar before, then you know he is one of the most physically dynamic speakers to ever set foot on stage! He'll get right up to the edge of the stage and dangle his toes off while he's talking . . . it really keeps that front row alert." Julie continued her live demonstration by running to the other side of the stage while saying, "Then he'll run across to the other side of the stage, get down on one knee just like this, point into the audience, and lower his voice (I didn't know she could get her voice that low) to make sure you're listening to the important point he's about to make. Suddenly, he'll jump up (she jumped up), and he's off again (she was off and running) . . . right back to the edge of the stage." Then she paused, looked out into the audience (I think she heard my tape on timing and voice inflection) and said, "I'm here . . . (then she pointed at me) to keep him from doing that!"

When the laughter subsided, Julie explained to our audience that I had fallen down the stairs in my home and had suffered a head injury that resulted in positional vertigo and that people with vertigo don't need to be running around and hanging out on the edges of stages. She went on to say that a second side effect of the head injury has been short-term memory loss and that even though she'd never heard me say anything from the platform that wasn't worth repeating (I really liked that part), we were using the new interview format to help me stay on track with the information I wanted my audience to have.

Then she came to stand by me, and with her arm around my shoulders she said, "At a time in life when most his age have long ago retired, my father finds possibly his most important work still ahead of him. He is willing to be transparent, and he continues to speak and write because he wants to show you that life on life's terms is still well worth living." Before she even sat down, I knew we were going to have a great time on stage together!

Jay Hellwig's prediction about how the audience would respond to the father/daughter interview format was right on. The audience could see and hear Julie's love and respect for me and my love and respect for her. If I did start to repeat myself, Julie easily redirected me, and we've had a very fruitful and comfortable stage partnership ever since.

The most common comment we get from individuals who have seen us together is that it is wonderfully encouraging to see a family that is as close and loving as ours. Several men and women have told us that they were so touched by our interaction and close relationship that they called their own fathers or went to visit them shortly after the seminar was over.

We've also heard from many individuals who say that seeing me press onward in spite of my obvious disability has inspired them to press ahead as well. For instance, after hearing me at a Get Motivated seminar, Megan Mellquist wrote that she had recently been diagnosed with a seizure disorder and lived in paralyzing fear that she would have a seizure while she was in the middle of making a public presentation: however, she said, "I am going to take a cue from you and live my life the way I did before I was diagnosed and stop living in fear, and if it happens, so what? At least I am not letting it take control of my life; I am going to take back control."

Based on input like the previous two examples, we knew something much bigger than we could have imagined was going on. The audience was relating my struggle to their own struggles. For years I'd read in the press after my talks that "of course it is easy for Mr. Ziglar to be enthusiastic and motivated, he's making lots of money from these highly energized talks he gives, but does what he's teaching really work?" Now it was obvious that my life was anything but perfect and I was as enthusiastic and motivated as ever. I could still profess, and the audience could easily see, that what I'd taught through the years does work and that it was, in fact, working overtime for me at that very moment.

Paula L. Reed—Another Name For Help

Thirty-plus years ago we met Paula Reed through our daughters Suzan and Julie. The three of them worked as waitresses at the Old San Francisco Steak House in Dallas in the midseventies. At that time Paula was pursuing her college degree to be a speech pathologist. The girls remained friends after all of them had left the restaurant, and Paula attended many of our family get-togethers and holiday meals since her family lived in another state. In other words, Paula became a very close friend to our whole family and is loved like one of our own.

We had been out of touch for a while when Paula attended a bridal shower for Suzan's daughter, Katherine, at my son and daughter-in-law's home. One day shortly after the shower Julie and Paula were talking on the phone and discovered that Paula and I had more in common than we realized! She, too, had suffered a serious head injury when she took a fall stepping from a boat to the dock. Like me, she had to completely "reshape" her life.

Paula told us that after her accident she was unable to organize her thoughts. Her ability to sleep was disturbed. She could not work in her field of speech pathology because she could not stay focused. She kept going to doctors, who gave her no direction on how to cope with or improve her cognitive abilities. But she pressed forward, knowing there had to be someone who would be able to diagnose her problem and know how to correct or make it better. Over time she met many people who were able to help her increase her mental capabilities. Ultimately, Paula discovered that head-injury patients need to be their own advocates or have advocates if they aren't able to pursue the best solutions for their circumstances. Her struggle inspired her to help others. I still believe that you can have everything in life you want if you will just help enough other people get what they want. Paula is a living example of that.

Paula spoke with and gave Tom some much needed hope for my future. My accident had burdened him with decisions I wish he'd never had to make as the CEO of our company. She told him she believed that my greatest words had not yet been spoken and that my head injury would force me to communicate in a different but possibly more powerful way.

It is my personal goal to live up to her positive expectations! Paula has spent countless hours helping me. Not surprisingly, the tools from her speech-therapy days have combined with the new information she accumulated to create activities to help me stay on top of my game. Second Corinthians 1:3–4 is working in both of our lives:

Blessed be the God and Father of our Lord Jesus Christ, the Father of mercies and God of all comfort, who comforts us in all our affliction, so that we may be able to comfort those who are in any affliction, with the comfort with which we ourselves are comforted by God. (NKJV)

So Many Care

I have been surprised at how many lives are touched by head injuries, and I have been blessed by the individuals who have reached out to me and my family with information about what has worked for them or their loved ones.

The position we found ourselves in was one in which it was critical that we keep strict control of everything I was doing in order to evaluate exactly what processes, procedures, products, treatments, etc., were being effective. We are grateful for the prayers and good wishes for a return to health and vitality and the sincere desire on the part of so many to offer aid, comfort, and suggestions for my recovery. I am filled with gratitude for those who are capable and willing to help me deal with my head injury and provide me with the knowledge I need to make good decisions. To be on the receiving end of such thoughtful kindness and love is humbling.

Enter My Best Friend

Nine days after Julie and I did our first on-stage interview together, Bernie Lofchick (Brother Bern), my best friend for more than forty years, came to Dallas to attend the wedding of my granddaughter Katherine Witmeyer. He was shocked when he saw how seriously the fall had affected me, and he instantaneously related my family's circumstances to the situation his family had faced years earlier.

Many of you will remember that I wrote about Brother Bern's son, David Lofchick, and the struggle he and his family had with David's cerebral palsy in my book *See You at the Top*. Brother Bern knows better than just about anyone that overcoming health obstacles is often a family project, and he was determined to fully enlist my family in the fight to regain as much of my prefall health as possible. With the exception of what we were doing with Paula, we had all gotten bogged down in the old-school approach of waiting passively to see if time would take care of my issues. Bernie's approach was anything but passive!

He took Tom aside to discuss some ideas about how to get me back on my feet and suggested we get a personal trainer to work with me several times a week to restore my strength and help me regain my balance. He also wanted us to find a doctor who was interested in solutions and who wasn't overwhelmed by problems, just like the one he'd found for his son David years before.

The day after Katherine's wedding, while Tom drove Brother Bern to the airport to catch a flight back to his home in Winnipeg, Canada, Brother Bern inspired him with this personal story:

> I grew up on a farm in Canada. I was four years old when my dad woke me up one morning at 3:00 a.m. "Kup," he said, "get up. We have to go down to the barn." Kup was my father's nickname for me. In German-Yiddish it means "the head," and in my family it was my father's way of calling me the smart one.
>
> When we got to the barn, a mare was giving birth to a foal.
>
> "Kup, what do you see?" my father asked.

"I see a momma horse having a baby," I replied. The mare was in trouble, and my father had to reach in and turn the foal.

"Kup, what do you see?" my father asked.

"I see a baby horse coming out."

"Kup, what do you see?" he asked again.

"I see a baby horse shivering on the straw."

"Kup, what do you see now?" my father asked.

"I see the baby horse trying to stand up and the momma horse licking it."

"Kup, what do you see?" my father continued to prod.

"I see the baby horse struggling to stay on its feet."

"Kup, what do you see now?" he asked.

"I see the baby horse trying hard to stand on wobbly legs and the mother nuzzling it."

"Kup, what does it mean?" he asked.

"Daddy, I don't know."

"Kup, it means that where there is struggle, there is life," he answered.

Tom replayed Brother Bern's story and its meaning over and over in his mind and ultimately told me and the Redhead the story and how strongly he'd been impacted by the idea that where there is a struggle, there is life. Tom said he had shared Brother Bern's story with Paula Reed, and they both thought we ought to set aside the book I was working on and make my next book about how I was embracing my struggle. I got so excited! Immediately I knew the wisdom of what he was saying and that my audiences would relate. I wanted *Embrace the Struggle* to be the topic of my talks and the title of the next book.

3

To Embrace Is to Accept

I began to think about the reason people had been impacted by my previous books, and I recalled the many letters I had received. Time after time they spoke of their struggles and how what I said or what I had written encouraged them and gave them hope. When you cut through all the motivation and inspiration, it was, and still is, about encouraging people to accept their circumstances and start right where they are to have better, more fulfilling lives. My story and the stories of those I have included in this book prove that people can face anything and be even more in their weakness than they were in their strength.

While it is true that it is easier to have a great attitude when everything is going your way, it is also true that the choice to have a great attitude is something nobody and no circumstances can ever take away from you. One day Jay Hellwig was driving me to one of my many therapy appointments when he asked me what had been difficult for me to adjust to since my accident. I allowed that not being able to get up and do for myself as well as I used to had caused a little glitch, but that I didn't spend time even thinking about that. Instead of thinking about what I don't have, I think about how lucky I am to have the Redhead looking after me, and my children working at and taking care of my company.

Complaining about my situation won't change a thing. It might run off some friends who get tired of hearing the same old song of woe, but embracing the struggle has the potential to change everything about the situation. You can complain, or you can say, "Well, now, this is a fact, so here's what I'm gonna do about it." My fall was just an accident. I was a little careless in my steps. That is all. I try to do the right thing in the right way, and that within itself solves a lot of problems for a lot of people. I make sure I respond to my situation, which means I'm looking for a solution, instead of merely react, which can result in complaining. One is positive and productive; the other is negative and futile and doesn't lead to a whole lot of good.

My mother, who never complained, was my first example of how to live life. She lost her husband and her thirteen-month-old baby girl within six days of each other. She was grief stricken, heartbroken, but she trusted God. No, she was not a complainer. Even with six of her remaining eleven children still too young to work, she did not complain. She didn't have any reason to complain because she never took anything into her own hands. She left her problems in the hands of God where they belonged.

Then Jay asked me how I got content with my situation. I told him that I never claimed to be content. I said I was dealing with it in what I thought was the appropriate way, recognizing the help that God was providing for me with friends and family. I still haven't missed a meal since all of this got started, and I'm still productive in my career, so, you know, I really don't have anything to complain about. But that doesn't mean I'm not going to do what it takes to improve my condition. I'm not content to accept the status quo when I can still do something to improve my situation.

I'm eighty-two years old, and that simply means that even if I'd not fallen down, I still wouldn't be able to do all the things I could do when I was thirty years old, so I don't regret what I can't do—I'm grateful for what I can do. As you know, one of my favorite quotes is, "The more you complain about the problems you have, the more problems you'll have to complain about; and the more you express gratitude for what you have, the more things you'll have to express gratitude for." I just believe that's the right way to approach life.

I can't walk and run as fast as I could. I can't climb the steps quite as easily as I used to. But, you know, those are such minor things; I just don't give that a thought. I'm grateful I can walk! I think of getting around as something I've got to do differently now. My life has had a change of direction, a change of priorities, and a change of what I have to do and what I get to do. This is who I am, and this is where I am. As a Christian, I even know Whose I am! I actually know where I'm going, and where I'm going is a lot better than where I am. And that is exciting, because I really love where I am!

I want each of you to understand by the time you finish this book that everybody has struggles, but you have a choice. You can either complain about 'em and say, "This is not right," or "This is not fair!" Or you can say, "You know, I'm grateful for the life I've had up until this moment; and here's what I'm planning to do, the best way I can, to keep my friends, keep my family, and keep the right attitude, regardless of what happens to me and regardless of what the circumstances are."

I think most readers identify with the reality that struggle is pretty normal. Setbacks are part of life. So now what we've got to decide is how we handle them. Realistically, we can say, "Well, you know, I'm not certain I'm gonna like this, but at the same time I've had a lot of good things happen to me, and I don't think this is going to be fatal, so I'll get my little note pad out, and I'll start taking notes on what steps I can take to solve this particular problem. Which of my friends can I talk to and ask for suggestions? Which of my mentors or teachers or family members who are trustworthy and knowledgeable and loving can give me some input? I wonder what the Bible has to say about this. Does my pastor have something that he could offer that would be helpful? What did I learn in school that might apply to my present circumstances? How many friends do I have who would resonate with what I'm going through and love me or respect me enough to offer some suggestions?"

All of us have more human resources than we utilize, and sometimes that's because we just don't want to bother them. In reality, a friend is somebody who is thrilled when you share a problem you have and ask for help. A lot of people respond to that, particularly if you have not had a dozen problems last week, last month, or even last year—in other words, if you're not a complainer. If you are a complainer, you might have already spent your help quota. But if you've always been fair and tried to help others, if you have a good relationship with people most of the time, if you're the right kind of person—meaning you're dependable and honest and trustworthy and have a good record of doing the right thing—you'll be surprised at the number of people who are pleased to offer suggestions, give you their thinking on what you can do, and help you in any way they can.

I really do believe that God has blessed me so liberally and so wonderfully that if I weren't grateful for my life, then nobody's got a right to be grateful. Of course, I recognize that things are never going to be as they were—so now I choose to express gratitude for what I still have, because I do have a lot left. I can still speak and write. I can still make friends. I still love and encourage others, and I can still set an example for people who have in many cases situations much worse than I have. Why, if I can't do something I've still got friends who do things for me. I even have friends who drive me around anywhere I need or want to go and a wife who still loves me completely. She's the only woman I've ever loved, and she still tolerates me and even encourages me every single day. Life is still good! So in my mind I just have so little to complain about that I'm not gonna complain about any of it.

If anything, this accident has brought the Redhead and me even closer. She's just been what she has always been, and that is very, very helpful and optimistic. She has done everything she possibly can for our benefit and our family's benefit. I thank God for her every single day—and the rest of my family. Like I say, I just don't have anything worth complaining about!

I'm doing the best I can with what I have and enjoying it in the process. When I get out on the golf course, which is seldom, and tee the ball up and hit it 125 yards, I don't say, "Oh, I used to hit this ball three hundred yards!" I'm just grateful that I can hit it as far as I can and am still able to get out there and enjoy playing. In my lifetime I've had one hole in one. I doubt that I'll ever make another one, but I have had that one, and it was a joyous occasion! Incidentally, since my fall my putting has improved—so there is an unexpected perk!

Because I'm eighty-two years old, I figure getting to sit down while I deliver my message is a perk as well. It was not difficult for me to accept this change, because the message is so much more important than how the message is delivered. If the message has reality in it, makes sense, and is helpful, then whether I'm sitting or standing, shouting or whispering, if the message is valid and sincerely believed, I am still able to make contributions to other people's lives.

I love to teach, educate, and encourage people. There is nothing as intriguing or exciting or gratifying as being able to give somebody a word of encouragement that makes a difference in his or her life. In fact, I continue to learn because I believe I have a responsibility, a calling, to be prepared to answer questions—I think that is biblical. I accept that it takes me longer to finish reading a book than it used to. But I also have more time to read a book than I used to. Truly, life takes care of itself to a very large degree, *if* you accept life on life's terms!

The One to Accept

I know my attitude about accepting life on life's terms exists because I have accepted the One to whom I owe my life, Jesus Christ. If you've heard me speak or read any of my books, you probably know that an elderly black woman named Sister Jessie led me to the Lord on July 4, 1972. I think one of the reasons I have such affection for my black brothers and sisters is because my mother taught us from childhood, "One day you will stand in front of a color-blind Lord . . . you will be kind and gracious to your black brothers and sisters."

You need to understand that I was born in Alabama and raised in Mississippi, two of the most racially prejudiced states in America during the time before racial desegregation, so my mother's attitude was almost unheard of. Had she been typical of her time, I would never have invited a black woman to spend the weekend in my home, and I might have missed out on knowing Jesus. Because I have accepted Jesus, when I face a struggle, the hill is not as steep and the climb is not as difficult. Christ said, "I am the way, the truth, and the life" (John 14:6 NKJV), and when you really think about that, when you've got that to hang on to—a Lord who loves you and gave His life for you, a Lord who is on duty twenty-four hours a day—it's such a comfort to know that you don't have to solve all your problems by yourself. I don't have to have all the answers. I rely on Him completely in every way. I ask for guidance, and He gives it to me. I get into His Word, the Bible, when I need help. I pray for His help, and I am always asking for wisdom, guidance, and direction so that I'll make the right decisions and do the right thing. I pray that you, too, have the comfort and joy of knowing Jesus as your Lord and Savior.

When Acceptance Is Difficult

As I said earlier, my most difficult struggle in life thus far has been losing my oldest daughter, Suzan. When she was seriously ill and it was obvious she was at death's door, we did a lot of praying. We asked God to spare our daughter if it was His will. We also sought all the medical help that was available. But as she got worse and worse, we had to accept the fact that the end was near. When she died, we were brokenhearted, but we trust God, so we accepted that He is God and He knows more about what should be done and what's best to be done, so we took comfort in our faith and His Word. This scripture was especially meaningful to our family: Isaiah 57:1–2—"The righteous perish, and no one takes it to heart; the devout are taken away, and no one understands that the righteous are taken away to be spared from evil. Those who walk uprightly enter into peace; they find rest as they lie in death" (TNIV).

Everybody has a time to go, and we have the comfort of knowing that Suzan is far better off in heaven than she ever had been here with us. But that doesn't change the fact that I don't much like life on those terms. Life without Suzan is not as good as life with Suzan. But I can't change anything. I mourned for her with all that I am. I still mourn for her. I expect always to mourn for her. I've accepted that, and I've given myself permission to mourn until the end of my time here on earth. Because I accept the fact that Suzan is gone and I will always miss her, I have the freedom to cry when I feel moved to cry. I don't struggle against the tears, because with them comes a degree of relief. I simply view each tear as a testimony of the love I have for Suzan and the gratitude I have for being given the honor of loving her and having her for my daughter. It is the best attitude I could find to deal with losing Suzan.

Accepting my fall and its consequences can't compare in any way to accepting the loss of my daughter, but choosing the best attitude in any situation has much to do with acceptance. If we stay riled up and in turmoil, always questioning "why" and visiting the "if" questions, we relive the pain of our emotions again and again. We get mired in the wallowing hole of self-pity or self-doubt, and our attitude becomes laced with fear, regret, and resentment.

If we accept that the past is the past, yesterday ended last night, and today is a brand-new day, we can have an attitude of hope. We can look forward to today with an expectation that it will be better than yesterday. Individuals who are able to embrace this concept are the ones who deal best with what life throws in their paths. They are the ones who have learned and accepted that they can't control everything that happens in their lives, but they can control their attitudes and choose how they respond.

I choose to accept life on life's terms, and, like my mother, I choose never to take anything into my own hands. I trust God to handle the unknown. There is an element of faith that is critically important to our ability to accept the struggles that come our way. If we can grasp the way God sees our circumstances, as we are told in James 1:2–4, "My brothers count *it* all joy when you fall into various trials, knowing that the proving of your faith works patience. But let patience have its perfective work, that you may be perfect and complete, lacking nothing" (LITV), and know in our hearts that the challenges of life hold as much good for us as the good things do, then we have His power at our disposal to move forward by faith. If we approach human misery from a human perspective, it will make no sense, but within the spiritual context of faith God produces the ability for us to embrace the struggle because He will be glorified when we do. I like the words of encouragement Gene Archer had for me. He said, "When you embrace the struggle, you embrace the Master." I hope you come to see the wisdom of the choices I have made and that you, too, know or find the kind of faith I'm talking about here.

Art Anderson

I've had the pleasure of praying for my daughter Julie's friend, Art Anderson. I understand that the issue I've been praying over is still unresolved, but after I heard what I'm about to tell you, I know God just has a different order of business. Art's story fits right here because he has embraced the Master, and God has been glorified. Art's story is vast, a book in itself, but I'm going to stick with what I think is possibly the most profound example of acceptance I know of.

Art Anderson deeply loves his wife and their seven children. It is not unusual for him to "pull out the stops" and drive hundreds of miles late at night to be with them, especially when one of the children is having a birthday, an event he has promised never to miss. It was his youngest daughter Inge's birthday on this occasion, and Art was determined to be there as promised. He was about an hour from home when he noticed something strange was happening to his heart and to his breathing. It was very mild, so he kept driving. Then it got worse, and he knew he had to get to a hospital right away.

He remembered there was a hospital in a town about fifty miles ahead. With the exception of one convenience store about eight miles outside of the town he was headed for, there was only dark wilderness on either side of the familiar two-lane highway he was on. Art was thanking God he had plenty of gas to make it to the hospital. He kept pushing forward harder and harder. He was feeling worse by the minute, and he figured he would die if he didn't get to the hospital very soon.

Just a few moments before he got to the convenience store, it occurred to him for the first time that he could kill someone else in his frantic attempt to save himself. Without a second of hesitation, he swung off the road and into the convenience store lot. He questioned if he was going to die because of his decision, but he made it out of his car and collapsed into the arms of three deputy sheriffs who were on coffee break. They immediately got an ambulance, and Art was whisked to the hospital that he probably would not otherwise have reached in time.

But Art faced yet another problem. During his ordeal Art lost his ability to speak and kept slipping in and out of semiconsciousness. He couldn't answer the nurse's questions or tell her about his experience while driving. The only information she had available was what the deputy sheriffs were able to relate. In his weariness and state of resignation Art said he kept thinking that he might never see his family again, and thoughts and images of his wife and each of their children kept the tears rolling down his cheeks.

Finally, the nurse took a different approach to her questioning and asked Art if he had any type of persistent medical condition. And indeed he did. Art had received a head injury in childhood that resulted in a partial complex seizure disorder, a form of epilepsy in which convulsive activity usually does not manifest in the violent bodily movements typically associated with epilepsy. Instead, the effects of Art's seizures are generally confined to activity within the brain itself. Art could only slightly lift his hand, but enough to point to his head, and he managed to get the word "seizure" partially said, at least enough for the nurse to understand.

Soon Art was wheeled to various lab and technician rooms where an MRI was performed as well as a number of other tests that he barely remembers. But all of them were negative for recent seizure activity. An otherwise routine electrocardiogram was never performed because heart trouble was not indicated, the emergency room was extremely busy, and no one had any reason to suspect a heart problem was the cause of his current condition. His vital signs may have been somewhat erratic and irregular, but that would have been attributed to the aftermath of whatever trauma he had sustained.

In the morning, after Art was fully alert, he explained his experience while driving the night before, but by then everything was back to normal, no official diagnosis was made, and Art was released from the hospital with instructions to notify his family doctor.

Art's wonderful wife, for whom he expresses great love and devotion, drove him home, where he apologized to his young daughter for missing her birthday. She hugged him, saying, "Daddy, you are my birthday." Later his car was retrieved from the convenience store, and the names of the deputy sheriffs were obtained so Art could write them thank-you cards. Nothing further came of the incident, and Art put it out of his mind and went on with his normal activities of life.

A few months later, once again Art was headed home at night, but this time he was on a four-lane interstate. The same symptoms suddenly hit him, but this time with greater force. There was total darkness all around, and he couldn't remember seeing any signs of an upcoming town that he hoped might have a hospital. He looked for lights in the distance but saw none. Frantically, he pushed forward, feeling death closing in.

"I have to find a town. I have to find a town. I have to find a town," Art kept telling himself over and over, *just keep pushing forward.* He was starting to feel disoriented when the same thought he'd had during his last event occurred to him: *If I keep driving, I might, and probably will, kill someone else.* Art also knew if he pulled off to the side, he would surely die. Again, without a second of hesitation, he pulled off the road and brought his car to a stop to await the inevitable. (In his panic, it never occurred to him that he had a cell phone!)

Art kept his headlights on, hoping the highway patrol would find him in time. He glanced ahead for a moment and thought he was hallucinating. Not fifty feet ahead of him in that seemingly dark and deserted area was a small exit ramp with only one sign. It was blue and had large white lettering: HOSPITAL. He eased up to it to make sure it was real and saw an arrow on the sign pointing the way. He followed a narrow road, which wound around a wooded area, and behind all the trees stood a big building that was bathed in light. He eventually made it into the emergency room, and in short order he was on an emergency-room table, hooked up to monitors, with a doctor and nurses and medical technicians all around him.

Art was conscious, and the doctor told him, "I think you've had a heart attack, but you made it through that. Now you're on the verge of a stroke, and we can't seem to control it." The doctor said several times, "You're about to stroke. You're about to stroke."

Then, suddenly and at the same instant as if it were choreographed, the doctor and other medical staff surrounding Art stepped back with a look of amazement. Art thought perhaps he had just died—until the doctor spoke with a tone of disbelief.

"I've never seen anything like this. All your vital signs instantly snapped back to normal."

The doctor's look of shock continued, but everyone else who had been tending to Art showed signs of relief and gratitude. Something strange, but good, had just happened.

Art was not shocked. He knew God had guided him there to be hospitalized and stabilized. The next day his treating cardiologist said, "If—no, make that when—this happens again, you will die." The doctor told Art to see a cardiologist immediately upon getting home and made a point of emphasizing the seriousness of Art's condition. As the doctor was leaving, he turned and said, "Mr. Anderson, I want to be very clear. I didn't say you might die. I said you will die." Art was given several injections of medication and a prescription to regulate and control his heart until he got to a cardiologist where he lived.

When Art arrived home, he contacted a friend who was a retired neurologist. He immediately arranged a cardiology appointment for Art the next day. Art arrived, more tests were run, and a second appointment was set up. But the very next morning the cardiologist called and said he had reviewed his case and test results with the cardiac surgeon in the cardiology clinic. They had concluded Art should have surgery as soon as they could arrange it with the hospital—perhaps the next day or the one following. Art, of course, opted for the first available time. Then he told his wife and their children.

Art is my kind of guy. He likes to get to the point—the exciting part—so he skips lots of details. However, he did skip one detail I think you should know: the surgery went well. Now we'll race ahead to the only two lessons that Art says are of any real importance.

One is the guiding hand of God. On the first occasion, Art fell into the waiting arms of deputy sheriffs. He never even hit the ground. The second lesson occurred to him later. Art knows that survival, or self-preservation, is supposed to be man's most basic instinct, but he can attest to the fact that it is not. Love of others is. Both times Art had heart problems, he chose to pull over when he realized he might accidentally kill someone in his efforts to save his

own life. And both times God approved of his choice. God had sher-
iffs waiting there, unbeknownst to them or to Art or to anyone but
God, to get him an ambulance. On the second occasion, God parked
Art in front of a lonely little exit ramp with one sign: HOSPITAL.

Art knows that sometimes God allows us to visit the truth that
the Holy Spirit has inside of us, despite ourselves. He has thought
many times about when Jesus proclaimed in John 15:13, "Greater
love hath no man than this, that a man lay down his life for his
friends" (KJV). Art says he realizes that Jesus was talking to all of us
and about all of us; that this is how we were made. This is His plan
for us. God implanted love in our hearts, but we chose to override it
with self-preservation, sometimes in very extravagant and self-
gratifying ways, at the expense of those we were meant to love. It is so
easy for us to forget the words of Jesus: "Whoever tries to keep his life
will lose it, and whoever loses his life will preserve it" (Luke 17:33
NIV), in which he says that we must lose the self if we are to gain ever-
lasting life.

Art does not pretend to exempt himself from the worldly instinct
toward self-preservation, but he always had the sense that all four
Gospels could be stated in one word: *love*. Yet it wasn't until he embraced and accepted willingly that he would rather die than cause
someone else to suffer that he realized, as he put it, "love is not all the
fluffy, good-feeling things we sometimes think it is. Before all else,
love is a commitment, and upon that commitment stands the ability
to make the hard decisions, the right ones, the ones born of love.
Jesus gave us the greatest example of love based on commitment
when He said, 'not my will, but Thine, be done' [Luke 22:42 KJV].
Way down deep, love is simply who we are because God is love, and
we are meant to be one with Him."

Art said he does not understand it any better than that, but he
understands it better than he ever has before. I know that Art is in-

dwelt with the Holy Spirit, because without the Spirit, humanity, in its sin nature, chooses self-preservation. As Art has rightly suggested, when God is within, a person chooses love.

Art's health struggle has positioned him to know God, and to know God within, as he has never experienced Him before. Not once have I heard Art being concerned about how he's going to get by with his heart problems. He knows God has that handled. As I said earlier, if we approach human misery from a human perspective, it will make no sense, but within the spiritual context of faith, God gives us the ability to embrace the struggle because He will be glorified when we do.

4

Transparency

One day my daughter Julie asked me if it was upsetting to me to have short-term memory loss. I told her that I honestly did not ever feel upset because I could not remember what I had forgotten. My life today is entirely in the present. That kind of focus has its benefits, but I have to say that without the Redhead to tell me where we're supposed to be and when, well, I'd miss out on just about everything.

Some might call what I just told you "being candid." I call it "being transparent." There is no sense in trying to act or pretend like nothing unusual is going on with me. Just a few minutes of conversation on some days is enough to reveal my memory problem. Other days I have considerably more clarity, and if we met and visited for even up to thirty minutes, I might seem like my old, prefall self. At least that is what my family tells me. I can't remember all that happened yesterday or this morning, but I can tell you almost anything you want to know about stuff that happened before the fall, and that is why I'm still able to be on stage with the interview format.

But I have to be transparent with my audience. Julie tells me there are times when I get "stuck in a loop" and keep going back to the same topic. She interrupts me, and I usually have a one-liner on hand to put the audience at ease . . . when you laugh at yourself the world laughs with you. If we hadn't told the audience in advance about my fall and about my memory loss, it could get very uncomfortable for them while they try to figure out what is going on. That's one reason I'm talking about transparency here. The other reason makes the bigger point.

The first person you have to be transparent with at all times is yourself. If you can't see what is going on with you, you can't see what needs to happen next. The alcoholic who doesn't think she has a drinking problem won't seek help. The workaholic who denies that twelve-hour workdays are too long won't take time off to see his child's soccer game. The perfectionist can't and won't relax, the morbidly obese won't get healthy, and the people who think they present a perfect picture to the whole world take themselves way too seriously. The list is endless . . . add a few of your own . . . maybe you'll discover something that applies to you.

I've known many people who have been told by more than just a few friends that they had problems, but until they were willing to admit their problems, there was no convincing them they needed help. Reality can be pretty hard to take, especially when dealing with it might require gut-wrenching hard work. I come from a generation that didn't talk about personal problems. You sucked it up and went on with your life. If things weren't going well, it was your duty to hide it from anyone and everyone. It didn't matter if your problem was marital, spiritual, financial, or emotional—you just didn't talk about it. You made sure that your neighbors and the people you worked with, played bridge with, and went to church with didn't find out how bad things really were at your house. Appearances were more important than getting help.

Speak with anyone who lived through the 1950s and you'll hear stories about the man or woman who "went crazy" and was seen running through the neighborhood without a stitch of clothing on. The mental hospitals were loaded with people who couldn't cope; and the shame you felt for knowing about something so personal, so private was palpable if you happened to be in the presence of a family member of the insane individual. In those times, the families of the mentally ill were shunned, so anything was better than asking for help and admitting there was a problem.

The Redhead volunteered at the mental hospital when our children were young. She and several of her friends went every other week to play bingo with the residents who were not dangerous. I'll never forget the day she told me in hushed tones, though we were in the privacy of our own home, that one of our neighbor's daughters had been admitted. I felt so bad for all of them, but to have called on them to see if they needed anything would have been socially incorrect. We were all bound to silence and keeping our distance. No one wanted to cause the family any more embarrassment than they were already suffering.

Leaving the Old Ways Behind

When I first started doing a lot of public speaking, I knew that what I said had to make a difference in people's lives or there was no sense in saying it. I instinctively knew that people needed to relate to what I had to say on an emotional and applicable level and that I had to be real myself if I wanted my material to make a "real" difference to the individuals who heard it. So I figured I would just tell it like it was.

I talked about the tough times early in my sales career when the electricity was turned off and when I had to turn a car back in to the bank because I couldn't make the payments. I talked about the times I only had a quarter for gasoline. I even told about not being able to get my wife and new baby daughter out of the hospital until I sold a set of cookware and could pay the sixty-four dollars we owed. That's the short list I told about, and to this very day that Redhead of mine tells me how uncomfortable she was with my telling the world about our financial woes. Interestingly, by the time I started speaking a lot, we were not in that kind of financial hot water, so I was referencing the past, but the Redhead still saw it as a negative representation of us. She, too, is a product of her generation.

Nothing, in my experience, has a stronger impact on individuals than hearing stories of how it was then, how it is now, and what happened in between. Those stories give hope to the hopeless. They say, "See, life can be hard but it will get better—if you do!" If you can't see the light at the end of the tunnel you can't see where to go. Stories of hope inspire people to find their way out of bad situations. Like the parables in the Bible—they give direction.

I've made it my business to compile the stories of the everyday man and woman. I attribute, to a very large degree, my ability to see how one person's struggle will inspire another to overcome their difficulty to the success I've had as an author and speaker. I owe much to the individuals who have allowed me to share their stories and struggles with the world. Their transparency is what has made the difference in the lives of the people who have seen me speak, read my books, viewed my DVDs or listened to my tapes and CDs.

Tamara Lowe is one such transparent individual. You may recognize her name because I introduced her earlier in this book as the cofounder of Get Motivated Seminars. She and her husband, Peter, have been a big part of my life for over twenty years now, so it made sense that they would be asked to give a taped interview to be presented at a huge, fund-raising eightieth birthday party that was given in my honor.*

There was Tamara, bigger than life on the big screens at the front of the ballroom, saying that when she was ten years old she began smoking pot, and by the time she was twelve she had dropped out of school. Tamara became a drug addict and a drug dealer. But all of that changed when she became a believer in Jesus Christ at the age of seventeen. She went on to say that the first book she read as a Christian was the first book I'd ever written, *See You at the Top,* and that she didn't have any idea that just a few years later, at the age of twenty-four, she and I would begin to work together, presenting seminars and influencing people positively from one side of this mighty nation to the other.

I was delighted as I watched and listened to this beautiful, successful woman of God reveal her troubled past to the hundreds who attended in order that she might encourage them, honor me, and give the glory to her Savior. I recently had the pleasure of endorsing her first book, *Get Motivated!*

On a similar note, since my daughter Julie has been traveling with me and doing the on-stage interviews, she has been asked to do some print and radio interviews about what it has been like to have me for a father. One of those interviews was done by Randy Welch (we turned the tables on him; see his story in chapter 9) for an online internet Christian magazine titled *A Time to Love, the Magazine of Christian Relationship Insights.* The article "Growing Up Ziglar" ran

---

* The whole birthday party was a surprise, as was the fund raising for the Zig Ziglar Center for Ethical Leadership at Southern Nazarene University in Bethany, Oklahoma. Go to www.ziglarcenter.com for more information.

in the March 2008 edition, and, though it held no surprises for me and the Redhead, it might have raised an eyebrow or two in the general readership. Julie spoke candidly about her struggle with alcoholism that ended more than twenty-three years ago.

I thought it was an exceptionally good article because it helped the reader see the grace of God that transformed my daughter's life. None of us is perfect, not one. Some of us are able to keep our failures more to ourselves; others seem to do everything, good or bad, with great public fanfare. When you happen to be the child of someone who lives in the public eye, well, you try a little harder not to be noticed. I believe that is why Julie's drinking problem was always below our radar. She went the extra mile to be sure her parents didn't know she even drank, much less had a problem with it.

As her mother and I told Randy when he interviewed us about Julie, she had already been sober several months before we found out she had a problem. I was disappointed when I learned that Julie had made the choice to drink, but it didn't change my love for her. We really don't "saw sawdust," and we were just grateful she had gotten her life back on track. The fact remains that Julie has been able to help and encourage many, many people who struggle with alcoholism. And with their blessings I have written about Julie's alcoholism, her husband Jim's alcoholism, and her daughter Amey's alcoholism in some of my previous books so that we all might encourage alcoholics and their loved ones.

We've had people remark that they just didn't think someone like Zig Ziglar would have children or in-laws or grandchildren with those kinds of problems. I, as you might recall, did not become a Christian until 1972. I was forty-five years old. By then Julie was a few weeks shy of being seventeen, and though we did go to church some as she was growing up, Julie did not have the benefit of being raised by a Christian father. I don't think she would have gotten so far off track if she had been raised in a family that had its foundation in Christ. We know Tom did not have the same struggles his sisters had, and the influence of Christianity is the only difference there was in how we raised them all.

I can assure you that being positive, having a good attitude, and looking on the brighter side of life does not inoculate you from life's problems. It does, however, make it a lot easier to accept and then work through the problems when they arise. The truth is, regardless of how you have raised your children, after a certain age they make their own choices . . . for better or worse. That's why you have to leave the children in God's hands too. That practice goes a long way to help you retain your peace of mind. I do want to add right here that Julie will tell you wholeheartedly that she *has* had the benefit of having a Christian father as an adult. It is never too late to do the right thing for your children—and yourself!

How Much Is Inherited?

I suspect you're probably wondering where all that alcoholism stems from. It does, after all, seem to run in families. Alcoholism has not been a problem on the Redhead's side of the family, and neither of my parents drank. I've made it no secret that I have a highly addictive or compulsive personality and that I credit God with keeping me from temptation of all kinds. Fortunately, I turned my tendencies toward the things that build people up instead of tear them down. But I, like so many others, had to learn some lessons the hard way!

When I took my first drink and realized I *really* liked it, a red warning flag went up in my mind. I made a mental note to be careful, and I avoided drinking too much. Not long after I became a Christian, I decided it would be best for me to quit drinking entirely since I didn't want to take the chance of possibly setting the wrong example. With one exception, when the Redhead and I were given complimentary wine in honor of our anniversary and I wasn't sure how to decline the drinks without being rude, I have stuck by that decision.

When I was a newlywed college student, I supported us by selling sandwiches around the dormitories at the University of South Carolina at night and was doing well. Then one night somebody suggested a little game of dice, saying he would roll me double or nothing for a sandwich. I agreed to it because I figured more people would buy sandwiches, thinking they might get them free.

Business did pick up, and I won about as often as I lost. Then one evening a guy challenged me to come back by his room when I finished selling my sandwiches and really roll the dice. I did and ended up losing nearly forty dollars. It was all I had, and I had to borrow money for the cab fare home. For me, that was a tremendous sum of money, and I could not afford that kind of loss, so I made the decision that never again would I gamble at anything.

I kept my word until many years later on the golf course—when I joined a threesome, and, as we were ready to tee off, they said they always placed a little money on the game, pointing out that they played round-robin so we would change partners every six holes. It wasn't a lot of money, but a lot of principle was involved.

Not wanting to be a stick-in-the-mud, as we would say down home, I went along, knowing that it was wrong because I was breaking my promise to myself. At the end of the first hole I knew I had made a mistake and should have backed out at that point. Thanks to the skill of the person I was playing with, we won that hole and would have won a small amount of money as a result. At the end of the six holes I had the worst six holes I'd had since I started playing the game. All I could think about was the fact that I had broken my word. I knew that I was doing the wrong thing.

At the end of the six holes, even though I was ahead, I explained that I was bowing out of the betting. I apologized to the fellows and asked them to forgive me. They were most gracious and laughingly said they would take my share that I had won. That's exactly what happened.

I've often thought about the number of times we go ahead and do something even when we don't really feel good about doing it. This inhibits our performance tremendously. My advice, therefore, is always the same: if you do what is right, you are always going to feel right about what you are doing. With integrity you do the right thing. Emerson said that "ability without honor has no value," and he was right.

All of this when added up simply means that if we do the right thing in our personal lives, the benefits will become part of our family and spiritual lives—which will become part of our professional lives. In short, it always starts with us.

Two-time Pulitzer Prize winner Barbara Tuchman said, "The number one need in America today is people who will accept responsibility for their own lives," and that responsibility includes doing right by others. Be honest first with yourself, and then you will have integrity with others.

Incidentally, after that golf game I've never participated in any way at any other game or anything else that involves winning something from another person.

I'm sure I could have gone my entire speaking career without telling anyone that I don't gamble or drink and why. I could have left out the truth about how many different jobs I've had in the course of my sales career; how many times I relocated my family in search of the pot-of-gold sales job. I could have skipped telling how my wife has cried with relief when I came home with cash and we could pay bills and buy groceries. But I could never have convinced you that you can improve your attitude and your circumstances if I couldn't show you how I'd done it myself!

I was young, vigorous, and healthy when all of the circumstance mentioned above happened. Now I have challenges that I may never entirely overcome, and I want you to see how having the right outlook, realistic expectations, and constant hope for something better will serve you and the people you love so much better than resigned acceptance of the status quo. Life is to be lived transparently, excitedly, with eager anticipation of the good things that still lie ahead, in spite of our circumstances.

5

Physical Struggles

Sometimes, even recognizing a problem can be a struggle.

Birth defects, accidents, or medical events that cause visible disabilities are immediately recognizable. You can tell they happened simply by looking. Addictions, learning disabilities, diseases like cancer and muscular dystrophy, Alzheimer's, attention deficit disorder, and conditions such as autism become apparent over time.

But while accidents and birth defects knock you flat with their sudden, unexpected appearance in your life, acknowledging the subtle signs that something might not be quite right with your new baby or someone you desperately love takes more time. You don't want to "guess" wrong or infer anything that might have devastating consequences for your loved one and for you.

Elizabeth Witmeyer

I've watched that dance of uncertainty in my own family. When my granddaughter Elizabeth was born, she was pronounced healthy and normal in every way. Her mother, my oldest daughter Suzan, had hoped for a sister for her first child, Katherine, and now the family was complete. But Elizabeth didn't reach the same milestones her sister had. She would fix her gaze on the nearest light and she avoided making eye contact. Holding her seemed to upset, rather than comfort her. Her behavior was anything but usual.

For three long months none of us dared to voice our fears. It was almost as if simply voicing our fears would make them a reality. How do you say to your daughter that you think her beautiful baby girl might have some problems? None of us confided in the other, and we later learned that we all held on to the hope that we were wrong and Elizabeth would grow out of the "phase" she was in.

By the time Suzan broke the ice and voiced her concerns to us, we all knew that Elizabeth wasn't "your average bear," as Suzan used to affectionately say. Every member of our family had utilized their built-in self-defense mechanism: denial. Denial serves as a coping device; it provides a safe place to hide the bad news until we are able to face reality. It allows your mind to gradually accept the unacceptable and is, at times, a blessing. But when denial is kept in place too long, you get the elephant-in-the-living-room effect. That's when virtually everyone in contact with the individual needing help sees the problem except for the primary caregivers and/or the individual. Everybody talks about how to break the news or help expose the problem so that something can be done to get help for the person in need. But everyone is afraid of hurting feelings or making loved ones angry for stating the unthinkable. Often, nothing is said or done until the person whose health and well-being is in question is in danger of one sort or another.

Fortunately for us, Suzan brought up her concerns before we had to, but that didn't mean everyone agreed with her. Her husband, Chad, initially thought she was being overly concerned about Elizabeth, and he clung tightly to the hope that time would prove him right.

After innumerable tests, the doctor told us that Suzan had come in contact with cytomegalovirus (CMV) during the second trimester of her pregnancy. The virus caused damage to Elizabeth's nervous system, which resulted in developmental disabilities and autistic tendencies. We learned that one in one thousand babies is infected with CMV in the womb, but only one in ten will have a negative outcome. Once we had the cold, hard facts, the mourning began.

Grief

The original hopes and dreams for the daughter, sister, granddaughter, and niece we had waited excitedly to meet and welcome into our family were dashed. Suzan had imagined that Katherine and Elizabeth would be close sisters, sharing late-night bedtime stories and giggling until she scolded them to go to sleep. She wanted Katherine to have the loving, fun relationship she had with her sisters. And instead, once Suzan and Chad died, Katherine would ultimately be responsible for Elizabeth's welfare.

When imagining what a child's or grandchild's future might hold, one thinks about the progression of that child's life. You visualize dance recitals or soccer games. In your mind's eye you see your little one all grown up in cap and gown, crossing the stage, hand extended to grasp a hard-earned college diploma. You wonder what her wedding gown will look like or if he'll marry someone as wonderful as his own mother.

News like our family got brings an abrupt halt to idyllic

thoughts and ushers in the pain and grief of what might have been. The fear of the unknown creeps into your heart and mind, and the struggle begins in earnest. The "what ifs" and the "whys" have to be marched to the back of your mind so that the "what nows" can be dealt with.

Questions about life expectancy and quality of life arise. For Suzan, the realization that Elizabeth would probably outlive her and Chad brought her to her knees. Her despair had never known such depths. Who would take care of Elizabeth? Would Katherine eventually be burdened with the physical and financial responsibility of Elizabeth's care? How do you plan to take care of someone well beyond your lifetime? Would Elizabeth be happy, healthy, easy or difficult, somewhat independent or entirely dependent?

Answers

One question led to another, and Suzan got answers. Before she died, Suzan's faith soared to new heights on the wings of Elizabeth's dilemma. She came to understand that God knew what Elizabeth's needs were even before Elizabeth was born. She knew that after she and Chad were gone, God would provide for Elizabeth like He always had. Suzan's peace about Elizabeth's future was total.

That doesn't mean that Suzan sat idly by. She threw herself into learning as much as she could about how to best care for her special-needs child. She got involved in the local MHMR (Mental Health/Mental Retardation) Center, and she found therapists and a school that catered to Elizabeth's needs. She did all she could to help Elizabeth reach her full potential.

After Suzan was diagnosed with pulmonary fibrosis, a terminal illness that can only be overcome with a lung transplant, she researched how special-needs adults adjusted to living in group-home environments. She had wondered if they were happier with that life-style than they were if they stayed in their parents' home until their parents died. She discovered that special-needs people adjust to new environments better when they are younger and that the social inter-action in a group-home setting often improves the language and social skills of individuals like Elizabeth. She immediately knew she wanted Elizabeth to live in a group home as soon as she was finished with the maximum amount of schooling she could have. New dreams for Elizabeth's future filled her thoughts.

Suzan died when Elizabeth was eleven years old. Ten years later, when her schooling was complete, Chad and Katherine helped Eliza-beth move into her new group home with nine other wonderful, fun-loving ladies. And, just as Suzan had anticipated, Elizabeth's language and socials skills have improved. She loves her housemates and espe-cially her house mother. They all love and dote on her, and she takes advantage of her position as the youngest in the house by teasing and joking with everyone and seeing how many of her chores she can get them to do for her. Suzan used to say that Elizabeth was "an exceed-ingly happy bear," and she still is. She visits her family often and stays busy doing volunteer work in her community. Suzan trusted God to take care of Elizabeth—and He has.

Logan Shannon

Michael and Tyra Shannon know firsthand about the tragedy of life-changing events. They know that the families and individuals touched by accidents or disease get immersed in the time, effort, and heart-ache that drive their struggle. But they also know the One who says, "Come unto me, all ye that labour and are heavy laden, and I will give you rest. Take my yoke upon you, and learn of me; for I am meek and lowly in heart: and ye shall find rest unto your souls. For my yoke is easy, and my burden is light" (Matthew 11:28–30 KJV).

Duchenne muscular dystrophy (DMD) is the devastating disease that the Shannons' son, Logan, now age fourteen, and his family struggle against. They could not and would not want to battle with DMD without claiming the comforting words of Jesus Christ, who promised to not only make their burden light but to carry their burden Himself.

The Shannon family experienced their life-changing event in September 2000 when Logan was first diagnosed with DMD. Though he was born with the disease, he did not show signs or symptoms until age five. For those of you who aren't familiar with DMD, one of the many different types of muscular dystrophy, it is a progressive muscle-weakness disorder that affects one in every 3,500 boys. It is mostly the result of heredity, but approximately 30 percent of the cases are caused by a mutant gene (just happens). Logan's DMD is the result of a mutant gene. The absence of the gene for the protein dystrophin keeps muscles from having an encapsulating membrane. The lack of this membrane leaves muscles unprotected, and they break down. First, the disorder aggressively affects the lower extremities, then progresses to the trunk and upper extremities, and finally affects the lungs and heart. Most boys die in their late teens and early twenties. It does not affect the brain.

Finally, a Diagnosis

Logan first demonstrated a general muscle weakness and had some difficulty with running. His father, Michael, a physical therapist, noticed the problems but felt they were developmental. His background in sports medicine and orthopedics hadn't prepared him to see Logan's initial inabilities as a red flag. The pediatrician told them every child develops at his or her own rate and not to worry or compare Logan to his older sibling. As time passed, more issues that could not be ignored arose. Michael and Tyra requested tests to see what the problem might be.

What stands out to them the most about the day they got Logan's diagnosis was how caring and how visibly grieved the physician was. She fully understood the disease and its progression, and she was devastated to be giving them the news. Michael and Tyra both look back and see that it was the first time of many that they saw a complete lack of hope in regard to Logan's prognosis. That obvious lack of hope gave them their first true understanding of how devastating DMD is, and they began to see the battle as man versus God.

Denial and grief followed the initial shock of Logan's diagnosis. It was only through prayer that Michael was able to give the problem to God and truly believe His Word: "With man this is impossible; but with God all things are possible" (Matthew 19:26 NIV). The Shannons honestly do not know how any family could deal with a situation like the one they face with Logan without the comfort of God in their lives. Yet Michael and Tyra both tell me they have repeatedly witnessed the lack of hope and faith in families and caregivers who are affected by this disease, so much so that the desire of affected families to help raise money to fund research for a cure is much less than you'd expect. Many, many people feel hopeless in the face of this disease.

Another event that clearly demonstrated lack of hope occurred during one of Logan's regular visits to his children's hospital. At each of his neurology checkups Logan was timed on how long it took him to run up the hall and how long it took him to get up off the floor. This time he sat on the floor for his test, and when he was told to stand up, he couldn't. His body had undeniably begun to fail. The Shannons knew his weakness had progressed and that he wouldn't be able to complete the task he was given, but the despair written on the doctors' faces reminded them that the doctors saw children with Duchenne from the initial diagnosis to the end stages of the disease and that the doctors' hope was securely centered on man and his ability to find a cure, not in trusting the outcome to the power of the one true Almighty God.

Michael Shannon describes best where he puts his faith and hope. "Logan brought me to my knees, and God kept me there. Prayer has become so significant to me in my growth as a Christian. I remember most of my initial time on my knees was focused on Logan. Now it involves so much more, and in a sense this was a gift from Logan. It was always there as a gift from God, but I never claimed it. Desperation has been one of the greatest gifts God has given us. We know what it is to be facedown, begging for the Lord's help, guidance, and wisdom."

Logan's condition has deteriorated tremendously since his diagnosis. He has needed an electric wheelchair to get around for the past five years, and this last year he experienced a dramatic loss of strength in his upper extremities. His parents and siblings have painfully watched the life of their son and brother being stolen from him one function at a time. A child who once could play and perform daily activities now is almost fully dependent on others for help. Logan lives each day struggling with the things most everyone takes for granted. He can't brush his teeth, lift a soda can, raise his hand in class, or even scratch some places that itch on his head. But the most painful of all is not being able to hug any longer because his arms are too weak. The Shannons tell me it rips your heart out to hear your child say, "I need a hug. Will you give me a hug?"

Life Is Not Stress Free

The Shannons say they would be lying if they said they simply deal with Logan's weakness and that is the extent of their struggles. Although they have given their struggle to God, that does not mean that the daily struggle becomes easier and their lives are stress free. Actually, at times things appear to be harder. In the last year, Logan has become hypersensitive to how things feel on his body. This may sound simple and straightforward, but it is far from it. If Logan feels an intolerable wrinkle in his pants, he can't do anything to fix it so he relies mostly on his mother, but also his father and siblings, to straighten it out. Sometimes it may take five to ten times of adjusting Logan's clothes or blankets to get them to "feel right."

Sleeping also has become a very difficult issue within the Shannon household. Logan wakes up between two and five times a night needing help adjusting his body, moving the blankets, scratching an itch, or rubbing a leg cramp. Tyra usually is the one getting up to assist him, and there are often other stresses that follow. First, lack of sleep can lead to irritation, frustration, and decreased patience for both Logan and his family. Second, consistent lack of sleep is unhealthy and can lead to more stress the following day, which leads to more prayer for strength and energy to carry on.

Michael and Tyra know many families have fallen prey to divorce when they have been confronted with similar trials. They thank God for the serving hearts that He has given them and pray that God keeps them strong in Him and never allows the breakdown of their family. They know the enemy of God would love to tear down their testimony and are grateful that Christ assures us in Hebrews 13:5, "I will never leave thee, nor forsake thee" (KJV).

Michael and Tyra asked me to consider this: "Have you ever been in a hurry, stressed from life's events, weary at the end of a long day, or lacked patience and a discerning spirit with your children? Throw in Logan's difficulties and his occasional frustrated attitude toward his condition, and the result is we fail. Even with our reliance on God we fail. Yet there is comfort in knowing that is why Christ came, lived, died, and rose again, because mankind has and will continue to fail. We acknowledge our failure to God, and through His love we repent and begin again. Our confidence in the Lord for His provision for this disease has gone from a state of mind that once was year to year, then month to month, eventually day to day, and now moment by moment resting on the sufficiency of His grace for our entire family."

There Is Gain

The Shannons see the positives that have come with the struggle. They are hopeful that Logan's siblings will gain wisdom, take on servants' hearts, and faithfully rely on God for all things as a result of their difficult situation. They spoke candidly about difficult but intimate moments they've been through with each of them. Last year son Devon, age twelve, recognized Logan's progressive weakness and approached Tyra, asking her in a troubled voice, "Is Logan dying?" How do you answer a question like that? She shared her heart and some specifics about the disease with Devon. Then, a little over a year ago the oldest child, Sydney, age fifteen, wanted to know more about what having Duchenne muscular dystrophy really means. Tyra and Sydney spent well over an hour in the van, in the garage, talking and crying over the truth of the matter. Up to that point, Michael told me, they had never shared the progressive details of Logan's disorder with the children. Their focus had not been on the problem but on God's sovereignty and power.

Soon, the Shannons will have to confront the concerns of son Corey, age ten. He prays every night for Logan to walk again and for doctors to find a cure for muscular dystrophy. They knew the day would come when difficult conversations would take place, and only by the filling of the Holy Spirit are they able to convey what their children's spiritual maturity levels can handle at the time. God has been faithful to meet them at their point of need each and every hour.

Mike and Tyra Shannon know there will continue to be moments in some days when they ask the questions: "Why is this happening to Logan? Why is this happening to our family? How are we going to get through this?" But they will continue to pray and praise Jesus during times of struggling as well as during times of blessing. More important, they will hold fast to God's promise: "Without faith it is impossible to please him: for he that cometh to God must believe that he is, and that he is a rewarder of them that diligently seek him" (Hebrews 11:6 KJV).

If you are the parent of a child with Duchenne or Becker muscular dystrophy or know someone with either disease, you might want to refer them to the Parent Project, an organization that has been a great source of help and hope for the Shannons. For more information go to www.parentprojectmd.org.

6

Financial Struggles

Financial struggles are often associated with health struggles, but they can also be the result of layoffs, downsizing, divorce, bad investment choices, poor money handling or irresponsible spending, getting fired, or companies going out of business. Some people are even born into a lifestyle that includes poverty and constant financial struggle and don't know life can be any other way. Regardless of the cause, people who are suffering financially are subject to depression and feelings of quiet desperation. The future looks bleak, and it is almost impossible to see a solution when you're living in fear of losing your home, your car, your credit, and your reputation.

We're going to look at several different sets of circumstances and see how people of faith have approached their difficulties and how God's hand was undeniably present in the midst of their struggles.

Back to the Shannons for a Moment

Before we get too far away from the story of Logan Shannon, I want to include what Michael and Tyra had to say about the financial struggles they have encountered as a result of Logan's struggle with Duchenne muscular distrophy. I am so happy that the Shannons are transparent and willing to share their entire struggle. Everyone knows that chronic illness or disabilities come with a financial cost as well as an emotional one. But many are remiss to mention the financial side of their struggle or even ask for much-needed help. I have been inspired as I read the Shannons' story, and I was glad to be reminded of what Michael says here: "As we strive to be faithful to the Lord, He tells us to prove Him and He will open the windows of heaven to pour out a blessing to us and there will not be room enough to receive it. Not only must we rely on God for spiritual growth, emotional stability, and physical endurance, but also financial support."

Michael went on to say, "God graciously made a way for us to build a fully accessible ranch home where Logan can drive around in his chair with freedom. However, we continue to face huge medical expenses along the way, which insurance does not always cover. Logan has need of a new twenty-five-thousand-dollar wheelchair that would accommodate his progressive weakness. For over a year our insurance company consistently reported that they would only pay 10 percent of the cost of the wheelchair, but we faithfully moved forward and ordered Logan's new wheelchair. God, as always in His timing, blessed us with another gift. We received the bill and the insurance company paid for 90 percent of the expenses!

We also need a new van and ramping system, but our biggest concern at the moment is making Logan comfortable enough to be able to sleep. We have investigated several beds that might alleviate his issues and believe that The Freedom Bed, a state of the art bed system recommended by a parent involved with The Parent Project, could be exactly what Logan and our family needs. Unfortunately, the cost of this bed is over forty thousand dollars and our insurance company has denied coverage. Along with regular medical bills and general equipment, these are just a few of the extra expenses that come our way. We would appreciate your prayers over these issues as well."

Michael knows from experience that the Holy Spirit moves people to be benefactors. Prayer opens minds and hearts, and it is also a place where our Father prompts us to contribute and help fill the needs of those He places on our hearts and in our paths.

Nothing Is Implied Here

Please don't misunderstand. I am not making a backhanded plea for anyone to send anybody any money. I am simply reporting facts, telling true stories, and talking about the harsh reality of financial difficulties that accompany health issues, lost jobs, accidents, theft, and acts of God like tornados, hurricanes, and fires, just to name a few. Shame has long been associated with the inability to pay one's debts, but everyone knows that there are circumstances beyond our control and that our financial security can change in an instant. The point I am making in this chapter is that when our lives are seemingly out of control, God is in control. He can and does provide, and oftentimes He provides in ways we could never conceive of.

Richard Oates

I have been watching in awe the incredible outpouring of love and financial support for my daughter Cindy and her husband, Richard

Oates. Richard was blessed to receive a liver transplant on May 22, 2001. His donor, Matthew McCord, was an amazing young man who had hoped that if he ever got to be an organ donor, the recipient would be a Christian so he could meet him or her in heaven one day. He will be meeting Richard one day, and we're obviously hoping it won't be anytime soon. Unfortunately, Matthew's perfect liver was undermined by a problem that Richard developed in his hepatic artery. Consequently, Richard was reevaluated and put back on the liver transplant list.

The past several months Richard has been in and out of the hospital. He was running an almost constant low-grade fever that spiked every three or four days, and he had been home sick in bed more than he had been able to go to work. If Richard didn't get to work, he didn't get paid, so the bills were piling up. He and Cindy had sold everything they could sell to get money to pay the bills. They consolidated debt, got rid of unnecessary expenses, and cut back as much as they possibly could, but there still wasn't enough money to cover their basic expenses without Richard's income. The stress was about to overwhelm Cindy, when her brother-in-law Jim Norman was prompted by the Holy Spirit to ask for help on Richard and Cindy's behalf. Jim was inspired by the following scriptures:

> *If a brother or sister is poorly clothed and lacking in daily food, and one of you says to them, "Go in peace, be warmed and filled," without giving them the things needed for the body, what good is that?* (James 2:15–16 ESV)

> *By this we know love, that he laid down his life for us, and we ought to lay down our lives for the brothers. But if anyone has the world's goods and sees his brother in need, yet closes*

his heart against him, how does God's love abide in him?
Little children, let us not love in word or talk but in deed and
in truth. (1 John 3:16–18 ESV)

Of course, Jim called Cindy and Richard and asked them to pray about allowing him to set up a website where he could tell Richard's story and ask for donations before he took any action. Cindy immediately knew that God was taking care of them, but Richard struggled almost as much with being able to accept help as Cindy struggled with the shame and fear of not being able to pay the bills. Richard was surprised at how much pride played a part in his initial "no-way" response to Jim's suggestion; but he came to terms with what was really driving his reaction, and he and Cindy both learned that it truly is harder to receive than to give.

The provision God has made for Cindy and Richard has overwhelmed all of us with gratitude, awe, and amazement. The blessings go so far beyond financial relief I'm not sure I can do justice in telling you what has occurred. But, as you might expect, I'm going to try—with a little help from Cindy. Here is what she wrote in a blog on the website:

> I cry tears of joy throughout the day as I think of the love that Rich and I are receiving. We don't deserve it. We didn't earn it. It's because of His amazing love that this is happening to us. That's the only thing that makes sense. To say that I am humbled beyond words is an understatement. The outpouring of love that Rich and I have received is surreal. I want to say thank you, but it seems so trite for the enormity of giving that we are experiencing. I have truly come to realize that we do not have a big God—He is HUGE! Thank you all for your "Amazing Love." The song

is on my lips on and off all day long. I have hope for the first time in a very long time. Thank you, thank you.

Jim compiled a list of family and friends and emailed them about the fund-raising project. He invited them to forward the email to others they thought might want to help or who would add Cindy and Richard to their prayer lists. The very next day funds started to arrive, and they arrived almost every single day for several weeks. Emails also started arriving with promises to pray and spread the word that more prayers and funds were needed. People Cindy and Richard hadn't seen or heard from, some for over thirty years, wrote and sent money. Perfect strangers wrote to say that God had impressed on them to donate money or to pray. Names of people Cindy and Richard had ministered to in the past appeared on the donors' list along with notes saying how wonderful it was to finally be able to give back and to help them in return.

God has used what seemed to be a sure disaster to show Himself all powerful to my precious children. They felt cradled in His loving arms, and they knew they were not alone in their journey to embrace their struggle.

It is with great joy that I tell you Richard had his second liver transplant on March 3, 2009. We are praying for the family of his donor and thanking God that Richard has another chance at life.

Sometimes It's About Business

I wrote in my book *God's Way Is Still the Best Way* about Michael Godwin and how he and his wife, Jayne, live their lives, both at home and at work, to glorify God. In a response to an email that my son Tom sent out asking specifically for prayer for me during my medical tests and telling about how I was embracing my struggle, Michael shared that he was having a struggle of his own. He epitomizes the heart we should all have toward the trials that we face. Here is what Michael had to say on the subject:

The term "Embrace the Struggle" is of special importance to me as our companies are presently experiencing great difficulties as a result of the deterioration of the financial and real-estate markets. We are doing exactly that. We are embracing the struggle. It is my goal to read James 1 every morning as a reminder of the pure joy that God has promised as we persevere through this time. What I've learned is that all of the fertile soil is in the valley, and it is in that fertile soil that the seeds of growth germinate. And you know what the best part is? As we ascend up the mountain, we do it with greater faith and wisdom. After all, what good is faith if you can't live it out?

Our company is embarking upon a mission to become a kingdom company instead of a company run by a group of Christians. We have set up a prayer room within our corporate office, and we are engaging in prayer before making business decisions. Our faith is growing exponentially as a result. This is our opportunity to live out our faith and show the way. For that we are grateful.

Michael sees the financial struggle as an opportunity! And it is! He reminds me of the eternal optimist who when he wears the soles off his shoes just figures he's back on his feet again. But Michael has good reason to be optimistic; he knows how big his God is.

No Money? Do This!

During the years of the Great Depression, when things were extraor-dinarily tough financially, I noticed that some people still wore nice clothes, drove nice cars, lived in nice houses, took nice trips, and even played golf at the country club. I have noticed the same thing in every decade of my life: regardless of the economy, there are some people who always thrive.

These people thrived because they understood one basic eco-nomic fact: while there was nothing they could do individually about the national economy, they knew beyond any doubt there was a lot they could do about their personal economy.

In regard to your personal economy, if you are unemployed, or if medical expenses, other unforeseeable events, or even just irresponsi-ble financial conduct have put you in a financial bind, I encourage you to hold a meeting with your family and take a look at your budget and financial reserves. Make a decision that without apology you are going to downgrade your spending dramatically. No meals out, no new clothes, no new car, no vacations, etc. Your entertain-ment is at home with your family. Get them on the same page with you. Explain that you know cutting back is hard but that you plan on doing everything possible to make certain that it is temporary.

Next, get in touch with your creditors, whether it involves a bank loan, a car payment, credit cards, etc. Drop them a note in the mail or, if feasible, visit them in person; explain your situation. Tell them that you have every intention of paying every dime you owe, but there is no way you can fully meet all of your financial obligations until you are once again on your feet. Enclose a check (even if it's only ten dollars), asking the creditor to bear with you, promising that you will continue to reduce the debt as quickly as you possibly can. Explain that your reputation and credit rating are extremely important to you and that you intend to fulfill your obligations. I have had to face this situation more than once, so I speak from painful experience. In each case the creditors granted my request and were cooperative. Ultimately, I paid everyone the full amount owed.

If you're familiar with my work, you know that I utilize experts in every field so that I can bring the best, most accurate information possible to my audiences. I've never been what you'd call a financial wizard (what you just read is pretty much the full extent of my financial knowledge), so I will defer to my trusted friend and financial expert Dave Ramsey on this one. You can learn everything you need to know about handling money, either the abundance or lack of it, from him. Dave knows from experience what Herb Caen meant when he said, "A man begins cutting his wisdom teeth the first time he bites off more than he can chew." Consequently, Dave is intimately familiar with debt and how to get out of it and has helped multitudes of people do the same. As a matter of fact, his people were instrumental in helping my daughter Cindy and her husband, Richard, downsize and get in a better position to deal with their financial crisis.

I want to share Dave and Sharon Ramsey's story of financial struggle with you because it was not brought on by a medical emergency, accident, or loss of employment. It was brought on by one of the most common ailments in America today: debt. If we're honest, we have to admit that we had at least some debt even before our crisis or our "suddenly" occurred.

Dave Ramsey built his wealth in the real-estate market. By the time he was twenty-six, he had a net worth of over a million dollars. But he also had incurred a tremendous amount of short-term debt along the way. After two and a half years of struggling to stay afloat, he and Sharon lost everything.

Thankfully, because Dave decided to learn from his circumstances, he gained wisdom . . . lots of it. And you know what he found out? He found out that he was his own biggest problem when it came to incurring debt and that if he could learn to control himself, he'd ultimately be in control of his money! One thing led to another, and today Dave's company, the Lampo Group, helps people who suffer from financial stress. As Dave says, "I've paid the 'stupid tax' (mistakes with dollar signs on the end), so hopefully some of you won't have to."

The mission statement of Dave and Sharon's company is: "The Lampo Group, Inc. is providing biblically based, common sense education and empowerment which gives HOPE to everyone from the financially secure to the financially distressed."

I know you fit the profile of Dave's mission statement because everyone, struggling or not, needs hope. So look Dave up at www.dave ramsey.com, and listen to him on his nationally syndicated radio program, *The Dave Ramsey Show.* What I love most about Dave and Sharon Ramsey is that they both put God first in their lives and their business. Let what they have learned the hard way minister to you and your needs in the financial arena of life.

A Hand Up

There are those who struggle financially even before they are old enough to know what finances are. They are born into poverty. My father provided for his family, but when he died there wasn't any insurance money to help us live comfortably. My mother was a wise woman, and she was able to grow food for us in her garden. She seemed to be "putting up" food year-round. Our few cows provided the milk we drank and that my mother churned into butter. We sold the extra milk and butter, and we raised chickens that provided eggs and much-needed meat. We were offered food, blankets and clothing by the pastor of the First Baptist Church of Yazoo City right after Daddy died. Initially, my mother said we didn't need charity, but when the pastor reminded her he was just doing as the Bible instructed, looking out for the needs of widows and orphans, she accepted his kind offerings. She often spoke in hushed tones of the sadness she felt for those who didn't have land to plant a garden or keep a cow . . . they were the truly needy during the time of the Depression.

For many years the welfare system, which was designed to help people through difficult times, has made the financial hole deeper and more permanent. Today it is not unusual for welfare to reach beyond the first generation of recipients to the second and third generations. I remember reading several years ago of a young person who wanted to get out of school and away from his family so he could get his own welfare check. That's a tragic goal to have. Thankfully, I've also met several people who desperately want to get off the welfare rolls. If they happen to live in Denton County, just north of Dallas, Texas, their chances of making that happen are greatly increased.

Jesus said in Matthew 26:11 that the poor will always be among us. He also instructed us in Matthew 25:40 to care for "the least of these my brethren" (kjv), and in Mark 12:31, "Thou shalt love thy neighbor as thyself" (kjv). A small Bible study group searching for the meaning of love was inspired by scriptures like these to found Christian Community Action (CCA). The original members of the organization wanted to be a conduit of God's love, and over the past three decades they have found ways to help the underprivileged help themselves financially and spiritually.

Since its inception on February 22, 1973, CCA has grown to serve over 12,000 people each year. More than 2,500 volunteers help in this organization that annually gives more than $1.1 million in food to families and provides more than 1,660 people with education and vocational training. Volunteer doctors help over 1,500 patients annually who use vouchers provided by CCA, and nearly $675,000 in prescriptions are distributed to those in need.

Christian Community Action learned that while people do need help with gifts like clothing, house repairs, etc., what they really need is financial help with house or rent payments, money for prescriptions, medical treatments, or utilities. Providing for their needs was going to require more than simply collecting items to be redistributed; it was going to require corporate donors and a revenue-producing resource. Corporations have stepped in to help, but the idea for starting a resale store has been the most profitable idea thus far.

Three CCA resale stores now provide 54 percent of the ministry's cash flow, or $5.5 million per year. Incidentally, another great side advantage is the 110 jobs (with benefits) that exist because of the resale stores. The money that is made through the resale stores is distributed to clients who have earned credits by going to classes that teach them how to live responsibly. Individuals learn money management through biblically based budgeting classes that are taught by volunteers. The volunteers have learned how to both show compassion and teach discipline as they run the day-to-day operations. They don't casually hand out their charitable gifts and aid—clients must present documentation of financial need. It's also a disciplinary process because missed appointments automatically result in forfeited aid, and vouchers are distributed only at the end of life-skill classes. Learning responsibility by being held accountable is a new experience for many recipients.

CCA is a charitable organization with compassion that deals with the physical, mental, spiritual, personal, family, and career aspects of lives. The financial is important, but the other areas offer the most long-term benefits. CCA, and other similar organizations, need our encouragement and support. Their success record makes many charitable organizations take notice of the biblical admonition to love your neighbors as yourself, but love them effectively and efficiently by giving them a hand up and not just a handout. Yes, CCA is making a huge difference in the lives of the people it touches and there are similar agencies throughout this great country of ours. Help is available.

God Will Show the Way

Trust God to meet your special needs in unique and wonderful ways. Let His people know when you are hurting and if you need help. If you know someone who could use the kind of help Jim Norman arranged for Cindy and Richard, help them. Be a part of the solution, and you'll get to share in the blessings. It really is true that you can have everything in life you want if you will just help enough other people get what they want.

7

Three Mothers, Three Struggles

Gail McWilliams, Kristi Brown, and Deborah all embrace their children physically; hugs abound. Each of them embraced the usual struggles that accompany motherhood, but individually they faced monumental struggles that would affect their children physically, spiritually, and emotionally. Each of them has a different story, but their motivation for seeing their struggle through to the end is exactly the same: love.

Gail McWilliams

I'll never forget the day I met a woman who sees life more clearly than most. I first met Gail McWilliams at what we at Ziglar, Inc., call

Monday Morning Devotions. Every Monday morning at 8:00 a.m. sharp we start our workweek off right by spending time hearing from inspirational, God-inspired guest speakers. Attendance is optional, and I'm extending an open invitation to any of you readers who happen to be in Dallas, Texas, to join us on any Monday morning with the exception of holidays. Go to Ziglar.com for our address: reservations are not necessary, so come at the last minute if you wish. You'll be blessed like I was the day Gail was our guest speaker.

Gail laughingly says that on that particular day she was grateful she could not see well because she would have felt intimidated if she had seen me taking notes as she spoke. By the time Gail finished talking, I had been impacted so deeply by the love of God that I couldn't see through my tears or speak when I attempted to close the meeting. It took awhile for me to find my voice, but her message was so strong and powerful that I was compelled to insist she write a book so the masses could be inspired as I had been. I'm pleased to report that she accepted that challenge, and one year later, to the exact date, Gail McWilliams placed her completed manuscript on my desk. I read it and gratefully wrote the foreword for *Seeing Beyond: Choosing to Look Past the Horizon.* In the first three months the book was carried to thirty-eight nations. It has now been reprinted and published in Spanish and is soon to be printed in Japanese, with other languages waiting their turn. I tell you this to show you that you don't have to wonder if you are in His will when God is behind what you are doing. His fruits are obvious.

I wasn't really surprised that Gail rose to my challenge, since she is a veteran of embracing the struggles of life, and she has done it with God's help. Interestingly, she was faced with a struggle that most women take for granted . . . having a baby. She and her husband Tony always wanted children. Gail says they know that every good and perfect gift comes from above and that children are like arrows in the hands of a mighty warrior, as stated in Psalm 127. They both strongly believe that having children is the greatest honor and promotion of any couple and that "their legacy and impact to affect future generations is limitless." But Gail and Tony's heart's desire was threatened by diabetes, a childhood disease Gail had. Her doctors said it was probably impossible for them to have children. Gail, however, chose to anchor her heart in hope and awaited the Great Physician's final answer.

Gail tells her story this way: "Our hope gave birth in time to five miracle children the doctors thought would be impossible for us to have. During my second pregnancy a pattern of risk to my eyes became clear. I had diabetic retinopathy. The blood vessels in my eyes hemorrhaged during pregnancy. The doctor surprised me one day with the ultimatum, 'Gail, you must choose today between your baby and your eyes.' I quickly said, 'I choose my baby.' The doctor stood to his feet as he angrily shut my file and said, 'What a foolish decision,' and then left the room.

"As I sat alone, stunned by his reaction to my choice and unaware of the winding dark road ahead of me, I remembered a passage of Scripture I had buried in my heart since I was a young girl. 'I have set before you life and death, blessings and curses. Now choose life, so that you and your children may live' (Deuteronomy 30:19 NIV). The giver of life had helped me make the right decision in the midst of the crisis."

Gail's decision for life for her unborn baby was not a struggle for her. She knew immediately what was right in God's eyes and that she loved her unborn baby even more than her eyesight. That she went on to have three more children is what I think makes this story truly remarkable. Each pregnancy created more hemorrhages in her eyes and brought her that much closer to blindness. But Gail trusted God and wanted more children.

Today Gail's beloved children are focused on living life on purpose—with purpose and for a purpose. Their personalities, diversity, and leadership skills, along with their musical talents, have caused those who know them and know Gail's story to be grateful for their lives. The daughter her doctor wanted her to abort has presented Gail with her first grandchild. She says that holding him validates what has always been at stake—the next generation. Gail believes life is the prize, even in the midst of the struggle, and that our choices impact others. She says few take a moment to see beyond their own lives to visualize the generations to come. When she holds her grandchild, she says, she can plainly see that something more has been birthed from her personal loss of eyesight.

Gail says that not being able to see the faces of her children and husband has caused her sorrow but that in the midst of what appears to be loss, she has begun to see in a world where most are blind. Gail says life is a gift and vision is more than just seeing. Though her eyesight is impaired, her vision became keen, and Gail assures me that when you have vision, you can see even in the darkest places of life.

Tears, prayer, and comforting scriptures have led Gail to unchangeable hope. For her, obstacles are opportunities, challenges are adventures. Faith is based on what is not seen, and faith has become her dearest companion. Gail has replaced self-pity with purpose and destiny as she has sought to see beyond the struggle. She says her struggles have not confined her but, instead, have catapulted her into a place of favor and purpose. Her desire to encourage others to see beyond their own struggles has led her to speaking nationally and internationally. Radio and television interviews and engagements have become standard, and she recently released her second book, *Engaging the Heart*.

I know you won't be surprised to hear that Gail's passion has always been in communicating with and encouraging others. God does give us the desires of our hearts, though His gift is often wrapped in packaging that doesn't resemble anything we ever would have chosen for ourselves. Once Gail struggled through the tears of self-pity and the feeling that her inability to see made her inferior and left her with a life that had no value, she realized that God, who delights in knowing the path of her life, had developed her personality to match her destiny. Everything that had happened to her up until that point was leading her to the purpose He has called her to.

I encourage you to look beyond the obvious for the way God has used the things you've struggled with to glorify Him. In the event you are currently in a difficult situation, I want to pray for you the beautiful prayer Gail McWilliams prayed for me and my family during our trying time. "May this dark place that your family has been walking be lit with His favor and peace. May you also understand that the dark place has not been because of abandonment or indifference, but simply the shadow of His wings."

Kristi Brown

Kristi Brown loves to sing. She has always loved to sing, and it was music that drew her to church. One day at Sunday school her teacher had a well-known picture of children gathered around Jesus. Five-year-old Kristi saw that there was a little blond-headed girl sitting right at Jesus' feet, and she said, "That's me! That's me!" She talked with her teacher about it, and that night, visiting with her mother, she accepted Jesus Christ into her heart.

At the time, her mother was single and Kristi's father wasn't in the picture very often, so when she accepted Jesus Christ as her Savior, she also embraced Him as her father. Even as a little child, the

Scriptures came to life for Kristi. She hung on Jesus' every word and cherished His promises of love and truth and comfort.

Her mother remarried when Kristi was eight, and her stepfather proved to be a wonderful man and an amazing father. Fortunately, church remained a constant source of comfort and support, and Kristi never missed a day if she could help it. She says her gratitude bucket is full because she had the benefit of growing up with a great pastor who taught her the Scriptures. As Kristi described the way she was discipled, I could mentally see the open Bible in her lap, the highlighter in one hand, and a pen in the other. (In my opinion, there is no better way to learn than taking notes and highlighting important points.)

Starting in middle school Kristi began journaling, writing out, and memorizing scripture from the front of the Bible to the back of the Bible. The love of music had attracted her to church, but the Word of God delivered instructions for life that Kristi could apply and use.

Like most young ladies, Kristi had an idea of what she wanted to do and be when she grew up. Unlike most young ladies, her plans for the future were jotted down on the back of an offering envelope. First she would go to college and meet the love of her life. Then she would marry, have four or five children, and be a stay-at-home mom. And, of course, she would continue to sing and do her music on the side. The future was full of promise, and Kristi went about her busy teen life with hope and a strong faith.

The summer Kristi was fifteen she attended drill team camp. A friend saw her reading her Bible and journaling and asked, "Kristi, why is Scripture so important to you? What is it about Jesus that means so much to you?"

The young lady was not a believer and her parents had just gone through a divorce. She was heartbroken and very angry. Kristi seized that moment to pray with her and continued praying with her for the first few nights. Then she began to simply tell her what Jesus meant to her and who He was in her life. Kristi started with John 3:16 and thought her friend was grasping all that she was sharing until her friend said, "Well, you just don't know, your life hasn't been like my life. You just don't understand." And she did not receive Christ at that time.

Kristi had had some tough things happen to her and her friend's remarks hurt, but inwardly she had to agree that what her friend was going through seemed bigger and harder than what she had experienced thus far. So that night she prayed that God would test her and try her, just like the song she loved to sing, "Test me and try me O Lord, examine my heart and know my mind." Kristi prayed, "God, I want you to test me. I do want to see what my faith is made of and why I trust you." She asked God to give her a testimony that would allow her to share with young girls and young women about Christ, and that her testimony would be so captivating it would create a desire in their hearts for a relationship with Jesus Christ. Kristi bravely challenged her own faith in that prayer and then waited to discover the answer.

The very next week, as Kristi was preparing for youth camp, she had a sharp pain in her side. Ultimately, a trip to the emergency room and a sonogram revealed the need for exploratory surgery. The doctors said they couldn't tell exactly what was going on, but they suspected cancer. What they discovered was a ruptured right ovary and considerable damage to the left ovary. Two months and several surgical procedures later the surgeon said, "Kristi, there's nothing else we can do." A complete hysterectomy was performed and sixteen-year-old Kristi's dream of being a mother was dashed.

Alone for the first time in the darkness of her hospital room, Kristi was overcome with fear and dissolved into tears. She went into the bathroom so the nurses couldn't hear her crying. And when she looked into the mirror to wash her face, the Lord began to speak to her. He said, "Kristi, there is nothing that you are going to go through in this life where I have not walked before you. My plan is perfect, and My steps are perfect, and I will carry you or I will walk with you through each road that I have planned for your life."

Six months later, a friend of Kristi's was extremely upset about what had happened to Kristi and demanded an answer to her question: "If your God is so good, why would He do this to you?" Kristi seized the opportunity to witness to her friend. She said, "You know, my God is so great and so awesome that He promised me that there is nothing that I'm going to go through that He has not walked the steps before. It seems that every step that I take leads me to the cross. And I look at Jesus Christ and His sacrifice that He made, and this is such a small sacrifice for me to make, and it makes it possible for me to share Jesus with you."

Two months later, as a result of Kristi's example of completely trusting the Lord and not harboring any anger or bitterness, her friend accepted Jesus Christ as her Lord and Savior. Kristi says she can honestly say that she never questioned, "Why is this happening to me?" She knew, because of God's promise that night in the hospital room, that it was His plan for her. She says, "He was the One that was writing the story, writing *my* testimony. I wasn't." Less than a year had passed since Kristi had prayed that God would test her, but she could see that He had done what she asked. He had taken what some might see as bad and evil and once again lived up to His promise in Romans 8:28 to use it for good. Kristi was truly called according to His purpose.

The years went by and Kristi attended Wayland Baptist University and was called to ministry. She began traveling and singing, and her testimony was her platform for witnessing to women.

The day arrived when Kristi began praying about her husband. The one thing that she questioned through all of her ordeal was who would love her. After all, the man she married would have to struggle with the same decision she ultimately had to make . . . not to have any children of his own.

Mister Wonderful arrived in Kristi's life via a mutual friend. They were having coffee after dinner on their first date when he told her it was his desire to one day adopt children and start a children's home. Kristi jokingly says that the heavens opened and a beam of light shone down on his head as he shared his heart's desire. She waited to tell him about her situation until she knew that they were falling in love. As hard as it was to tell him, she wanted to be sure he understood the sacrifice that he would have to make. His response to her was, "It's no question . . . and it's no sacrifice. I love you and I want to spend the rest of my life with you!"

Darrin and Kristi married and began ministering to single adults and young couples. About four years into their marriage they decided they were ready for children, but the cost of adoption was a huge concern for them.

As God would have it, just a few weeks after Kristi shared her testimony at a women's conference, a young mom called her (who happened to be the same age she was when she had her hysterectomy) and said, "I'm interested in talking to you about adopting the child that I'm carrying. Would you come and meet with me?" So Darrin and Kristi met with her and two months later their daughter Kendall was born. The most precious thing about Kendall's adoption was that they were able to help this young mother who had fallen away from her faith draw close to God once again.

Kendall grew into a talkative three-year-old, and one evening at the dinner table she started talking about her little brother. Kristi said, "Kendall, you don't have a little brother." And Kendall said, "I'm going to!" So they decided right then to update their home study. They turned in the last notarized statement required for the update and got a call twenty minutes later from the director of the children's home. She asked, "Kristi, are you sittin' down?" Kristi responded, "Actually, I am." And she said, "Well, that's great. You're gonna be a mom in an hour." Kristi exclaimed, "An hour?"

Darrin had just come in the room with Kendall, and Kristi said, "Congratulations, Dad!" He asked, "What?" and Kristi announced, "You're gonna be a dad in an hour!" Little did they know that it was a boy. His birth mother was incarcerated at the time and had heavily abused drugs and alcohol, which had done a lot of damage to her body. The birth mother told Kristi and Darrin that she believed with all of her heart that God allowed her womb to heal so that she could provide a child for them. Then she placed Cole into their arms.

When Kendall was seven years old she presented a lot of pocket change to her parents and said that she was saving her money for her orphaned sister. They told Kendall they would pray with her about her desire for a sister. A week later, a friend called about hosting an orphan Ukrainian child in their home for twenty-one days through an organization that facilitates orphan educational camps in the United States. They prayed about it and then pulled up an email on the computer that showed pictures of the children attending summer camp. Kendall said, "Mom! There she is! There's my sister!" And she pointed right to thirteen-year-old Nadia's picture. Kristi said, "Well, Kendall, we need to wait and see." They didn't even know if she was one of the children that needed a host family. Sure enough, she was. A week later Nadia was in their home. They fell in love with her immediately and are now pursuing her adoption.

When asked if she ever regrets praying the prayer to find out how strong her faith was, Kristi says, "No. I never do. I never do. I have never regretted that prayer, and as I look into the eyes of my children and at our pictures of our sweet Nadia I am reminded daily of God's promise. I see God's promise because had I had my own children and physically been able to do that, I would not have the children I have today, and that was God's plan for my life. I have no regrets."

Deborah

One of the greatest blessings I've received as a result of being an inspirational/motivational speaker is getting to meet people who share with me how something I've taught has changed their lives or the lives of their loved ones for the better. Such was the case when Julie and I spoke in Washington DC in September of 2007. We had finished our interview session and were walking away from the stage when a radiant woman extended her hand to me. I quickly told her I don't shake hands with women. I only shake hands with men, but I hug women. She graciously allowed me to hug her and then began to explain why she wanted to meet me in person. Her story is one of trials and tribulation, but also of victory and overcoming the struggle. Her transparency will bless many who recognize themselves in what she has written. I am grateful she has allowed me to include her story in this book.

In her desperation to be loved, Deborah had rushed into marriage with a man she barely knew and suffered terribly for her indiscretion. Two months later and with a baby on the way, her attorney husband told her, without an inkling of concern, that he no longer wanted the marriage and announced that he would not help her financially. Deborah was humiliated when she learned what everyone else seemed to have known all along . . . he was leaving her for a previous lover who was also an attorney.

Deborah had already had one child from her first marriage

when she married Harold. Now she was devastated but fought through her humiliation for the sake of her unborn child. Harold bounced back and forth from Deborah to his girlfriend; and before the marriage was finally, once-and-for-all over, Deborah had given birth to their daughter and later became pregnant with their son. Her self-esteem plummeted each time Harold left her for the other woman, but Harold's abrupt and final departure two weeks after she announced her latest pregnancy made her wonder how she would provide for her three children while she fought off depression and the demons of despair, anger, and frustration. She felt that she had failed her children and failed herself. She had, after all, brought them into the world and was responsible for them financially, mentally, and spiritually.

Deborah believed God was angry with her. She berated herself and suffered spiritually because she had not abided by her religious beliefs when she married and became unequally yoked to a man who did not believe as she did. Deborah had a deep-seated anger toward Harold that was killing her mentally and tearing her up inside; but as badly as she wanted to let go of the anger, she didn't know how to because she had forgotten how to pray. But God had not forgotten Deborah.

Fortunately, according to Deborah, she had the best parents in the world, and they helped her out with her money problems. Help came from another source too. A girlfriend invited Deborah to attend a seminar on motivation and offered to pay her way. When she arrived at the venue, she loved the energy in the air, the excited chatter that filled the room, and the smiles that seemed to be everywhere she looked. She had never attended a seminar on motivation and didn't know what to expect, but she knew she felt good being around people who were upbeat.

Deborah said when the event started they announced that Zig

Ziglar was to be the main guest speaker, and upon hearing my strange name she immediately began to wonder if she was in the right place. Then she said I burst onto the stage with excitement and started telling stories about my hometown, the Redhead, and my children. I'm proud that she was listening because I happen to know that those were the things I was talking about. But she said what really hit home with her was when I started talking about *Raising Positive Kids in a Negative World*. I talked about children and spiritual matters, and Deborah said it made her take inventory. She knew she was a good mother, but at times she wasn't sure she was doing all the right things.

I suggested that children should not wake up to an alarm clock in the morning, but to soothing music. I said they shouldn't be rushed and hurried up, because it would get them off to school in a tizzy. I explained that a fast bowl of sugary cereal would not serve them well throughout the day and that parents should be spending time with their children while they ate healthy meals or they might find themselves spending time with their children in dire circumstances at a later date.

Deborah went on to say she knew she had to have my audiocassette series on *Raising Positive Kids in a Negative World*, which was being offered at a discounted seminar price that day, so she borrowed the money from her friend. She listened over and over and implemented what I suggested. Her children had always been important to her, but that day they became her number one priority. Deborah didn't have time to be worried about what their father was up to—she had to mold her children and bring them up with a positive outlook toward life, no matter what.

Many years have passed since Deborah attended that seminar. Today Deborah is the mother of four wonderful children, and her new husband, Benjamin, is "the most wonderful husband in the world." She says, "He loves my children like his own," and she no longer struggles with self-pity or doubt.

She credits me with her success and the outstanding success of her children, but I know good instruction, unapplied, does nothing to create change. Deborah implemented what she learned, and the results were phenomenal. She taught her children the importance of being respectful, upright citizens, and they never gave her any reason to worry. She told me her children excelled in everything they did. They focused, put their minds on the task in front of them, and reached for the sky.

I hear the struggle of the single mother quite often. If you are a single mother, I want you to note that Deborah was a single mother when she was instilling life-winning values in her children. How your children turn out is not a result of the amount of money you have, but a result of what you have invested in them. Time, love, and godly instruction bring results everyone can be proud of. And just to prove my point, I'm going to tell you what Deborah's children have accomplished.

Her oldest daughter is a graduate of Briarcliffe College and works with the U.S. Department of Homeland Security. Her youngest daughter is a graduate of Howard University in Washington DC. Her oldest son is in his second year at the University of Maryland (UMBC), and her youngest son is an honor student at Polytech High School with a consistent 92 percent grade average. Deborah has every reason to be proud of her children.

I can't thank Deborah enough for taking the time to come talk to me in Washington DC. It is my joy when I get to hear of struggles overcome *and* hug my sister in Christ all at the same time. Deborah, in Yazoo City, Mississippi, vernacular, "Ya' done good!"

The Road

The roads each mother travels with her children are vastly different. Different children have different personalities and different needs. Their choices and struggles are as varied as their personalities, but how a mother directs, encourages, challenges, and responds to her children molds and shapes them for their futures. The mothers whose stories I covered in this chapter are just a few examples of how God does give the strength, the power, and the way to those who know Him. He is in control even when someone loses his or her sight of Him, as Gail McWilliams did. He is in control when no end appears to be in sight, as was the case with Deborah. And He is in control when tears on the darkest night wash away dreams for the future, as was the case with Kristi Brown. So remember, when you can't see your way through your struggles, God can. Let Him guide you.

8

From Addiction to Service

I touched on addiction briefly in chapter 4, but the topic there was transparency. I happened to use the stories of Tamara Lowe and my daughter Julie, both of whom are very candid about their past addictions, and I even wrote a little about how blessed I've been to recognize potential addictions and stop the behavior before it became a problem. But in this chapter on addiction I want to inspire hope in the group of people I see as possibly the most frustrated, exasperated, and exhausted group of all, those who love an addict and those who are addicts. People on either side of addiction struggle so hard, and it seems like the struggles that go along with addiction just pile one on top of another for years on end.

There is little more difficult than standing by as those you love barrel down a path of self-destruction. They often leave a wake of destroyed relationships, ruined credit, damaged property, and unfinished business in their paths. But the most awful side-effect of an addict's out-of-control behavior is the fear the addict's loved ones live with . . . that the addict will die or take his or her own life before help is sought. No one can prepare in advance for the disappointments, the lies and manipulation, the emergencies, the total upheaval and uncertainty that come with loving an addict. Learning how to "let go and let God" and keep from enabling an addict is, as they like to say in Alcoholics Anonymous, a process.

On the other side of the struggle is the addict. He or she is much like the apostle Paul, who said in Romans 7:15, "I do not understand my own actions [I am baffled, bewildered]. I do not practice or accomplish what I wish, but I do the very thing that I loathe [which my moral instinct condemns]" (AMP). They hate themselves, their lack of control, their deceitfulness, the way they disappoint everyone, and how their best intentions are never enough to keep them clean and sober. They have tried to quit and can't. Can't everyone see that?

The truth is, an addict isn't going to give up his or her drug of choice until the consequence of doing that drug hurts more than the benefits they think the drug has been giving them. That is, unless Jesus takes their compulsion from them one day at a time or even supernaturally, which many a recovered addict can attest to. Addicts can and do reach their "bottom." For some, their bottom is death, but for others getting to the bottom just means there is no other way but up—so up they go.

Fortunately, the following stories about John Plank, Pam, and Preston Dixon don't stop at the bottom. They do go clear to the bottom, but this chapter wouldn't be about embracing the struggle if their stories ended there. These stories will inspire hope in all who read them, because these folks have a calling today they could not possibly fill had they not been to the bottom and back.

John Plank

John Plank was a "two-fisted drinker." He drank from early morning until he'd pass out at night, and he drank that way for more than twenty-five years. Fourteen hospitalizations, four of which were court-ordered committals, didn't convince him he ought to quit. Like many "functioning" alcoholics, John was able to make some good money, and he lived for what money could buy. He says he was 100 percent materialistic.

You can imagine how devastated John was when his health failed and his wife decided to divorce him. John knew he was going to lose everything he'd ever worked for, and physically there would be no way he could work hard enough or long enough to replace even a fraction of what he was losing.

John was fifty-five years old when he found himself living in the storeroom of the small "mom and pop" restaurant he owned. He'd lost most of his colon and surprised everyone by surviving a second emergency colon surgery. He arrived back at his storeroom bunk only seventy-two hours out of intensive care with a colostomy that he was too weak to deal with and no desire to go on. His employees brought food to his bedside, but John just didn't want to live as he was living.

John says he was a sick person. He was sick spiritually, physically, mentally, and emotionally. He was, he said, "a believer." He believed in God, but he didn't have a relationship with Him and wasn't serving God in any way, shape, or fashion. He was a "worldly" person. It simply didn't occur to him to call on God when he was writing his two-page suicide letter to his son that Saturday night.

A home health care lady came by the restaurant Sunday morning to change John's bandages, and as she stood up to leave, she reached out and touched John and said, "Mr. Plank, God is going to take care of you." He thought she had lost her mind. He was about to commit suicide and she was talking about God!

But something happened when that woman touched John. He got the most uncontrollable urge to go one block up the street to a church where he didn't even like the pastor. John had run out of the back door of his restaurant many times trying to avoid the old white-haired man who had been sticking his head in the front door, asking, "Are you blessed today?" John didn't like "those Bible thumpin' Christians," and that is exactly what Pastor M. L. Milton was. John didn't understand why he suddenly felt he just had to go to that church, but he hurriedly (well, as fast as you can go when you're hurting from surgery) found clothes he could get on over his surgical site and ended up wearing an old pair of sweatpants, an old loose-fitting shirt, his gray sweater, and bedroom slippers since he couldn't bend over to get his socks on.

John had to walk only one block to get to the church, but he hadn't walked a block since his surgery. He got so dizzy halfway there that he had to stop and recover before he could go on. He said, "God, get me to that church!" and, indeed, he made it—to the last pew. After he'd sat there for a few minutes, watching all the people standing and raising their hands above their heads and singing praises to the Lord, he thought, *Lord, what am I doing here?* He thought the singing was never going to end, and it wasn't long after M. L. Milton began to preach that John thought, *When is this man ever going to shut up?*

By his own admission, John says he can't remember a single word the pastor said until he got to the very end of his message and said, "If there's anyone here today that would like to change their life, these altars are open. It doesn't cost a dime to give your life to Jesus Christ." And when John heard that, he came up out of that pew and ran, yes—ran, to the altar. He fell to his knees, and though he says he didn't know what he was doing there or how to pray, he lifted both hands into the air and with tears streaming down his cheeks said the shortest prayer that man ever says, "Help me, Jesus; help me, Jesus." And John Plank has not been the same from that day until this.

That night a lady from the church brought him his first Bible, and John began to read and study. He'd never read or studied anything in his whole life, but he had an uncontrollable desire to learn what was in the Word. About two months into his conversion, he was sleeping and woke up to a voice that said, "Study my Word. Go into the streets and the prisons of this nation and preach truth." John thought he was losing his mind!

The very next morning his pastor stopped by the restaurant, and John took him to the back room and said, "M. L., as soon as I close here this afternoon, you and Mother Milton drive me to Wichita Falls. I gotta go up there to the doctor because I'm losing my mind." M. L. looked at John and asked, "What makes you think you're losing your mind?" John said, "Well, I'm hearing voices." M. L. asked, "Well, what did you hear?" Trembling with fear, John told him what had happened. M. L., with relief etched in his voice, said, "You haven't lost your mind, John. God just called you to preach! You'll start Wednesday night." John told M. L. he hadn't even finished Genesis yet and that he couldn't preach, but M. L. would have none of it. He told John that all he had to do was tell the people what God had done to change his life. And he did.

I expect you'll be mighty surprised to read that John didn't quit drinking right away. No, John was an addict, true to his beer. He believed what he now calls "the devil's lies"—that it took a twelve-pack of beer to help him sleep through the night. He even argued the sleeping point with God when the topic of his drinking finally did come up, but he went ahead and asked to be delivered from alcoholism anyway. God did as he asked, and John slept like a baby that very first night. He hasn't had or wanted a drink since.

During the first year of John's ministry he learned that prisoners needed Bibles, so he started a fund-raising campaign. He painted coffee cans white, taped a request for money to buy Bibles for prisoners on the cans, and put them by the cash registers at gas stations, restaurants, and businesses. That year his ministry placed over ten thousand Bibles in prisons throughout Texas.

Today, nine-plus years later, John is a certified volunteer prison chaplain. He expects to serve in the neighborhood of 290 times this year, but he says the main thing he is called to do is love the incarcerated men with the love of Christ. He spends time with them one-on-one in their units, the areas where they sleep and live.

John's struggles were intense and all seemed to fall on him at once, but he survived the surgeries, the divorce, the alcoholism, the loss of his restaurant, and other "things." John Plank has been blessed to the core. He traded materialism for faith. Instead of serving customers, John serves the Lord, and he does it with his loving new wife who also has a heart for prison ministry. Together they serve God and marvel at the wonderful life they lead. John's story is what Romans 8:28 is all about.

Pam

Pam was fourteen years old when her mother introduced her to alcohol and turned her into her drinking buddy. Drugs like Black Mollies, speed, and diet pills were soon added to the list of things Pam and her mother ingested together. It wasn't long until Pam dropped out of high school and left home to get away from the physical and verbal abuse her angry mother directed toward her. She bounced around, living in different people's homes, looking for love and what life was supposed to be. Her struggle was well under way.

When she was almost seventeen, Pam got pregnant, and her mother sent her to live at the Edna Gladney Home for Unwed Mothers. She delivered a little boy and, at her mother's request, put him up for adoption. She returned to live with her mother and met her first husband shortly after at a Mexican restaurant where she was a waitress.

They had children: a little boy and a set of twins, and then they lost their last little girl six months into the pregnancy. Pam did not do drugs during this time, but she did drink a lot when her husband, who did not have a problem with drugs or alcohol, would let her. One day her husband decided he was going to go his way and she could go hers. Not knowing how to handle her problems, Pam turned to alcohol more and more and ended up leaving the children for her husband and his mother to raise. All she had to show for ten years of marriage was a pickup truck and an escalating problem with alcohol.

For two years Pam lived in that pickup truck. She found a stray dog one day and moved him into the truck to keep her company while she drank and drugged herself into a stupor. She knew how to dampen the pain and grief that defined her life, and each day brought more of the same.

Then she met her second husband, Tony. He introduced Pam to cocaine, crack cocaine, and other drugs she hadn't tried before. Two children and ten years of physical abuse later, Pam had had all she could take. She took her two children and went to a shelter on the south side of Forth Worth, Texas. There she met another man, moved in with him, and landed in jail for a bunch of outstanding tickets she had. While she was in jail, Child Protective Services investigated her, charged her with child abandonment, and put her children in foster homes.

When Pam got out of jail, she began flying into angry rages, was violent, and losing control of her actions. She was living on the streets, in vacant houses, in abandoned trucks, and in cardboard boxes that she tried to set up like a real home. She says she would get drunk, pass out, and wake up "with big ol' rats around me."

Pam was beaten up many times and once left for dead by a group of gang members. She vividly remembers being in the hospital and overhearing a police officer saying, "Well, it's just another prostitute, it's just a Jane Doe." She thought she might be dying and nobody would ever know who she was. She had truly lost her identity in the bottom of a bottle and the high of a drug.

Pam eventually served eighteen months in jail for the child-abandonment charge and another six months for another charge, but she returned to what she knew best when she was released: the streets and making her drug and alcohol money as a prostitute. One night she happened to see herself in a mirror at the dope house where she was, and her image struck her. She did not recognize herself. The questions came to her in a rush, "Dang! Who are you? You look awful! Where did Pam go?" Pam says she doesn't know what it was, but something changed in that instant. She was walking down the road that same evening, and a police officer arrested her for prostitution. She didn't even mind that she was going to jail. She says she "just knew something was going to be different."

That happened on August 16, 2001. About eight weeks later, on October 7, 2001, Pam was reading the Bible in her jail cell. She says she wasn't really looking for the Lord or even asking Him to help her. She was reading John 8:3–11 when "all of a sudden an angel (vision) of the Lord just appeared and showed Himself to me. It was so real I knew that Jesus had come for me. This was Jesus, and He had come into my jail cell to make Himself known to me so that I could be free."

Pam says in that instant she knew what Jesus wrote in the sand when he was talking to the men who wanted to stone the prostitute, because He was writing it to her. She believes He wrote, "You know, you're not guilty in my eyes." Jesus showed her that if she repented of her sin and asked Him to forgive her, she would not be guilty anymore. He would free her from that place (of guilt and shame). That night Pam had dream after dream of the Lord showing her the awful things she had done, the different sins she had committed, and with each revelation she would confess and say she was sorry. It was like she was on stage and watching a video of everything in her life, but it was just she and the Lord watching.

The next morning Pam says the Lord told her to look in the mirror and "tell Pam you love her." She thought to herself, *Okay, here's the first thing He's telling me to do, and I'm telling Him no.* Pam didn't feel like she loved herself, but when she looked in the mirror anyway, she saw the eyes of the Lord looking back at her. She was able to say, "I love you," even though she didn't understand what it meant. She just knew everything was going to be okay.

That's when she had her first talk with the Lord. She said, "You know You've made Yourself real to me. When I get out of this jail, I don't want to go back on the streets. I don't want to be homeless anymore. I don't want to lust for a man, and I don't want to be on drugs. I want to be free. I want to be able to walk a right life however You want me to do it; just make me able to do it."

On December 16, 2001, when Pam was released from jail for the last time, she made a beeline to Beautiful Feet Ministries, a place where she endured many a sermon in order to qualify for a free meal when she was homeless. For the eight years Pam had lived on the streets, the people at Beautiful Feet had been praying for her, encouraging her, and trying to show her a better way. Pam went there because even though she knew for herself that Jesus was real, she didn't know who He really was. She only knew "of Him." She was thirsty to know more, and arrangements were made to help that happen.

Pam went into a residential program called Fort Worth Teen Challenge, a twelve- to eighteen-month discipleship program for women over eighteen. She learned who God is, what He is about, why it is necessary to repent, and why you have to ask the Lord for forgiveness. She was being given the foundation for living. Eventually, she was encouraged to begin the healing process of discovering what had caused her to drink alcohol and take drugs. She had to face the pain and hurt that she had tried to hide and cover up with substances. She had to forgive those who had hurt her and recognize that what she had been searching for all along was the love of Jesus.

Pam graduated after twelve months in the program and became a full-time volunteer. She says the Lord blessed her with ten dollars a week so she was able to meet her needs and continue living on campus. Two years later Pam was asked to work full-time as a staff member, teaching women what she had learned. Right now Pam teaches Scripture Memory and how to make God's Word come alive. She also teaches how to take on the character qualities of Christ and gives the example that she was at one time a habitual liar. God took that sin out of her and showed her that she "didn't have to be afraid to tell the truth anymore, because the Truth is in you."

Pam's struggles have changed. Instead of wondering how she'll eat, where she'll sleep, and where she'll find her next high, she struggles in a positive way to know her heavenly Father better and to be obedient to His Word. She's not immune to struggles in the future, but God has honored her by giving her every single thing she asked for in that talk she had with Him when He revealed Himself to her in jail.

Pam lives "right." She is grateful her mom got to see her clean and sober and living for Jesus. She couldn't get over how different Pam looked. And Pam still marvels at the fact that she got to stand up and speak at her mother's funeral. Another blessing Pam has had is that five of her children are back in her life and only her son that she gave up for adoption is unknown to her. She takes care of one of her granddaughters at her home, and she is getting to tell her about God's love and teach her the moral basis for how to live life. Pam is changing the destiny of her family by breaking out of the mold of addiction.

Preston Dixon

Preston Dixon grew up in Dalworth, a small close-knit community within Grand Prairie, Texas. His life was uncomplicated, almost innocent by today's standards. His parents, Myrtle and Albert Dixon, loved him and encouraged him in all he did. They raised him according to Proverbs 22:6, which says, "Train up a child in the way he should go: and when he is old he will not depart from it" (KJV).

Preston was also blessed with athletic ability. The coaches at Grand Prairie High School thought so much of his talent that they put him on the varsity team his sophomore year. He proved them right when he became Sophomore of the Year for the Dallas–Ft. Worth Metroplex. Eventually, their star running back won a scholarship to North Texas State University (NTSU), now known as University of North Texas, in Denton.

Life up to that point had been anything but a struggle. All the good things seemed to come to Preston Dixon easily, naturally. But the very things that gave him so many advantages as he was growing up put him at a disadvantage when it came to knowing how to handle the faster pace of college life. The small-town boy did not fare well in the big city of Denton, Texas. The downward spiral of Preston Dixon started with a separated collarbone. Suddenly, he didn't have to show up for practice every day, and he began to meet a different type of person on campus. Preston is quick to say that he is the only one responsible for the choice he made to drink their alcohol and smoke their marijuana; nobody forced him. Those two gateway drugs soon led to snorting, sniffing, and smoking cocaine.

Interestingly, Preston was able to continue playing football even though he was kicked out of two dorms for smoking marijuana. Nobody seemed to care that he had a drug problem, so he stayed at NTSU, playing and using, for four and a half years. By the time he left the university, he was so hooked on drugs that he didn't go to class, he'd pawned everything he had, and he used his last dime to support his habit. He left the university without a diploma and with a lot more than he'd bargained for. An addiction to crack cocaine is no small thing.

Preston says, "They say crack kills, and it does. It kills your family; it kills your relationships; it kills your self-esteem; it kills your desire, and it eventually wants to kill you! One hit of crack is too much and a thousand hits aren't enough." He knows because the need for a thousand more hits drove him to steal from his own mother. He'd even run into stores, take merchandise, and dash back out if he thought he could do it without being seen.

But Preston was seen, and caught, so many times that his misdemeanor charges converted to a felony through a process called "enhancement," and that is how petty theft to support his drug habit landed him in state prison. Preston's parents had sent him to drug rehab several times, and he'd been to AA, but he just couldn't stay clean and sober. But in prison Christians mentored, loved, and prayed with him. It was there that he saw what happens to men who don't repent and change their ways. It was there in isolation, where Preston couldn't reach out to anybody but God, that he had his greatest life-changing moment. It was while he was imprisoned that he was set free.

Preston is grateful to God that he had nothing when he left prison. God's provision for his needs made it possible for him to "know" that God was directing his path. Upon his release from prison, God impressed someone to give Preston a car so he had transportation. When Preston told Pastor Denny D. Davis at the church he was raised in that he felt he was being called to preach, Pastor Davis said that he knew Preston's past and that he wanted Preston to spend the next three years proving his faith. Preston did as he was asked. And after he was ordained to preach in 2004 Pastor Davis told him, "I want you to learn now. I want you to go deeper and I'm going to pay for it." With his financial needs met, Preston enrolled at D. Edwin Johnson Theological Institute, and the Lord started opening doors for him to preach and share his testimony.

About a year later Preston was asked to officiate at the funeral of a good friend of his at Mount Gilead Baptist Church in Italy, Texas, a small town about forty miles outside of Dallas. One thing led to another, and Preston Dixon was called to the ninety-five-year-old church to pastor the two hundred-plus members full time. Preston Dixon—a man who says God gave him the gift of talking so much so that he can talk a cat off the back of a fish truck—is "peacock proud, hyena happy and elephant elated" to be serving the Lord with that gift every day of his life.

Comfort

John Plank, Pam, and Pastor Preston Dixon take comfort in knowing that from the ashes of their lives the Lord has made beauty. They each give back freely out of repentant and joyous hearts that know the power of God's healing grace. The light of the Lord seems to shine brightest when it comes from those who have been in the darkest places.

The people who love John, Pam, and Preston are blessed as well. They are relieved to have relationships with them that were impossible to have when they were using. When God restores one addict, He restores an entire family. If your family has a practicing addict, I suggest you go to a Celebrate Recovery or Al-Anon group near you. The help you get will give you peace in the midst of your addict's addiction. If you are an addict, go to a Celebrate Recovery or Alcoholics Anonymous group. The help you need can be found in either or both of those places. God will meet you right where you are. Embrace your struggle by taking the first step—do it today.

9

Lives Changed Instantaneously

Every day, all over the world, old people, young people, even babies, experience life-changing events. No one is immune from the possibility that the life one knows today could end today. Ask the man who just got a diagnosis of prostate cancer, the woman who fell through the ceiling, the man whose heart failed him, or the man who went into a coma what they had planned for the day, week, month, year, or lifetime before his or her world changed in an instant.

Because I have experienced a sudden, life-altering event like the individuals in this chapter have, I can tell you with full faith and confidence that it is possible to prepare for the unexpected. Yes, we can prepare for the struggle in advance. God never promised that we would have an easy, struggle-free life, but He did promise in Psalm

91:15 that we would call on Him and He would answer us. He said, "I will answer him: I *will be* with him in trouble; I will deliver him, and honour him" (KJV emphasis added).

In 1 Peter 4:12–13 the Bible says, "Beloved, think it not strange concerning the fiery trial which is to try you, as though some strange thing happened unto you: But rejoice, inasmuch as ye are partakers of Christ's sufferings; that, when his glory shall be revealed, ye may be glad also with exceeding joy" (KJV). Those who have been through a fiery trial say that although they wish not to go through it again, they would not trade for anything what they learned and what they know as a result of the trial. They see how God used their tribulation to mature and strengthen them and to bring glory unto Himself. They are blessed to be recipients of the exceeding joy Peter speaks of. They also know the peace Jesus left with us (see John 14:27) and that through patience He comforts us with scripture (see Romans 15:4 KJV). When you study and know His Word, when you hold it close to your heart, He speaks to you through it, and you will remember His promises when the unexpected happens and the struggle begins.

On my best day as a speaker and author, I could not reach or positively influence a segment of my audience who thought I could not relate to their predicaments. I was healthy. I was traveling and speaking to audiences all over the world and enjoying things many people would never experience. How could I understand what it meant to be disabled? Would I really be so excited about life if I had to struggle every day just to walk from one place to another, or if I couldn't remember what I'd done yesterday or what I needed to do today? God is allowing me to encourage those who can now know that I *do* understand. I *can* relate. And I am still positive, excited, enthused, and looking forward to what God has for me tomorrow, as are the people in the stories you are about to read.

Let me introduce my friends and encouragers: Mike Powers, the man who got prostate cancer; Pansy Kennedy, who fell through the ceiling; Randy Welch, whose heart failed him; and Charles Keith Hawkes, who fell into a coma. Two of them have for all practical purposes recovered fully, but a couple of them have struggles to contend with daily because of their life-altering events. All of them are grateful to be where they are today, thanking God and marveling at His unending grace.

Mike Powers

I first met Mike Powers in 2003 on the telephone. I was scheduled to speak in Madison, Wisconsin, and Mike, who has been the host of the afternoon program on Christian radio station Life 102.5 since that time, called me for an interview. He explained that his five-hour program (weekdays from 2:00 p.m. to 7:00 p.m. central time) was a mix of music, comedy, and information, but that the point of all of it was the importance of faith in God through a personal relationship with Jesus Christ. He seemed like such a nice fellow that I wanted to meet him in person, so I invited him to come to the venue, where we visited after I finished with my presentation. When Mike thanked me for letting him interview me, I thanked him! I am completely aware that without people like Mike Powers I would not be in the position I'm in today! I could only reach a fraction of the people I reach if it weren't for radio, TV, and the press, so I'm always grateful for the time and effort those in the media put into interviewing me.

The second time I was interviewed by Mike was shortly after my book *God's Way Is Still the Best Way* was published in 2007. We had a great visit, and I introduced him to my daughter Julie, who has assisted me on radio and press interviews (as well as the stage since my head injury). The two of us filled Mike in on my fall and all that had happened since. When we said good-bye that day, I figured I would speak with him again when my next book came out, but he sent me an email in response to the update and a request for prayers for me that Tom put in our company newsletter. Mike promised to pray for me and my recovery, and that's when he let me know that since we'd last spoken he'd been facing a struggle of his own.

The table was turned when I asked Mike if I could tell his story in *Embrace the Struggle*. Fortunately, he agreed. Mike told me he went to his doctor for his annual physical shortly after we'd had our last interview. The doctor told him he was in pretty good shape, but he was concerned about Mike's PSA level (prostate-specific antigen—an indicator of possible prostate cancer) being a little higher than normal. He said he wanted to do the PSA test again in a few months to be sure there was nothing going on.

The next test results arrived a few days before Christmas and indicated Mike's PSA levels were even higher. His doctor decided to send him to the urologist and tried to reassure him by saying, "For someone your age, prostate cancer is not normally something we have to deal with, but just to make sure, I want to have you checked."

The urologist checked Mike over, decided to perform a more definitive test, and used the ultrasound scan. He discovered that Mike did have prostate cancer. Mike discovered that "the words 'you have cancer' are very, very, imposing indeed!" Mike spent a lot of time in prayer and with friends and family. He discussed his treatment options with the doctor and ultimately decided the best way to eliminate the cancer, if it was still localized, was to eliminate the prostate.

Mike entered the hospital on February 26, 2008, and had the surgery. Over the next several weeks he began to feel more normal, and on April 8, 2008, Mike received the better-than-good news that his PSA test was normal. His 2009 test shows that he is still cancer free!

You may be thinking that's a pretty open and shut story. Mike gets the bad news, gets the surgery, and he's good to go. But Mike can tell you that "there are certain things in life that make us really, really question and wonder *Is God there? Does He care? Is He concerned about my health and well-being?*" Mike had plenty of time flat on his back to talk to the Lord, and some well-known healing scriptures helped him greatly. He shared them with me, that I might share them with you.

Mike points out that great words of encouragement are written in the Bible about healing and about how we can be well. For instance, Romans 8:32, "He that spared not his own Son, but delivered him up for us all, how shall he not with him also freely give us all things?" (KJV). "Surely that includes healing," Mike says.

This verse gives hope to those in the middle of a struggle: Isaiah 40:31, "They that wait upon the LORD shall renew their strength; they shall mount up with wings as eagles. They shall run, and not be weary; and they shall walk, and not faint" (KJV).

Mike assures us that Psalm 34:19 comes with a wonderful promise: "Many are the afflictions of the righteous, but the LORD delivereth him out of them all" (KJV). And that promise is that the Lord delivers us from not some of our afflictions, but from *all* of them. In Jeremiah 30:17 Mike was encouraged when he read, " 'I will restore health to you, and heal you of your wounds,' says the LORD" (NKJV).

Mike says those particular scriptures were very important in the healing process for him as were the wonderful prayers and encouragement of so many of God's people who rallied together to pray for him. I can assure you that is a huge number of people since Mike is on the radio daily speaking to a Christian audience, and I know he was transparent with them about his cancer and his surgery. He had much the same experience that I had with people calling and sending emails to let him know they were continuing to pray for him and that we have a sovereign God who holds us and our futures in the palms of His protective hands.

Mike Powers has been given a new lease on life with a new way of seeing. From start to finish his cancer ordeal lasted about half a year, but what he learned from it will last a lifetime. I'm already looking forward to the day he interviews me about this book. We'll both have a lot to talk about, and I expect gratitude will be at the top of the list.

Pansy Kennedy

Speaking of emails . . . I received one from a fellow member of Prestonwood Baptist Church in Plano, Texas, that included several of my favorite thing: *acrostics!* I love acrostics. I love reading them and dreaming them up. I use them to keep my mind sharp and to help me remember long, drawn-out stories or ideas. And I love anybody who goes to the trouble Pansy did to give me a word or two of hope. In AA they have a saying about sharing your "experience, strength, and hope" to encourage others struggling with similar circumstances, and that is exactly what Pansy did when she told me about her fall.

Pansy's fall wasn't down stairs like mine. No, she skipped the stairs entirely and fell out of the attic, through the ceiling, and onto the floor below. It happened in April of 1999 when Pansy was visiting at her mother's house in Louisiana. Her left foot simply slipped off the attic floor and down she went.

She broke her left collarbone, a couple of ribs on the left side, dislocated ribs on her right side, and got five stitches to sew up a gash on her head! And that doesn't count the extremely sore back muscles that even now occasionally remind Pansy of that day long ago.

It was quite an ordeal! For six days Pansy had to be helped out of a chair. For over five weeks the pain was so great that she couldn't lie down on the bed to sleep. She successfully staved off sneezes for thirty-seven days (imagine how a sneeze would feel with broken and dislocated ribs), but on the thirty-eighth day, one came on so fast that there was no stopping it—and with the horrible pain came relief as her dislocated ribs popped back into place. Finally, Pansy could sleep in bed again.

By week six Pansy was losing her patience. She felt as if she would never get over the pain and regain her strength so she could return home to her life in Dallas-Ft. Worth, so she decided to have a huge pity party and threw herself fully into the effort. Pansy cried out to Jesus, "You never had a broken bone. You don't understand!" Immediately the Holy Spirit reminded her Jesus was crucified. Pansy learned at that moment the excruciating pain she had endured did not begin to compare to how Jesus suffered on the cross for her.

That was probably the hardest lesson she learned, but it was far from the only one. Pansy also learned that her Father in heaven was always going to take care of her and that the collarbone is the one you prop the telephone on. She wouldn't expound on the last lesson but did say that God assured her of His provision, His pain and grace, *and* His sense of humor. Those insights helped her to endure the trials she was facing and led her to conclude that there are three reasons we go through trials and struggles:

1. to make us stronger
2. to make us more dependent on the Lord
3. to help others down the road

I concur with all three. I also found a great deal of truth in the acrostics Pansy sent me, and I'm not about to pass up the opportunity to share something I love. Here they are for your enjoyment:

TRIALS—True Revelation in a Low Situation
FOLLOW—Finding Our Loving Lord's Optimal Way

LISTEN—Learn in Silence Their Extraordinary Needs (Pansy's personal favorite)

SOLDIER—Serving Our Lord Diligently in Every Respect

With an attitude like the one Pansy has, her struggles are sure to be dealt with. I appreciate her transparency about her frustration and how she took it to Jesus. Struggles are frustrating and tiresome, and who can we cry out to if we can't cry out to Him? Thank you, Pansy, for "helping me down the road."

Randy Welch

Randy Welch was used to being in control. As chief information officer for the city of Garland, Texas, he was responsible for all the computer telecommunications and the staff that helped support them. The first time he missed work for heart issues was to repair a heart valve that wasn't functioning properly; he wasn't off the job long. The second time, well, Randy didn't have any control over that!

In March 1999, two years after he had his heart valve repaired, Randy started having problems with shortness of breath and stamina. He couldn't walk from the parking lot to his office without having to stop and sit down a couple of times. That's when he decided to see the cardiologist. She subjected him to a variety of tests and procedures but waited until his last visit to do the treadmill test. The longest Randy could stay on the treadmill was about a minute. That's when she told him they wanted to put him in the hospital and run even more tests.

The cardiologist was always straightforward with Randy. She said, "You know, I'm not sure, but you may need a heart transplant." Randy thought, *Yeah, right.* He checked into the cardiac intensive care unit (CICU) at the hospital on Monday morning, and the testing began. On Thursday they told Randy all the tests indicated that he needed a transplant, and they called the family together to tell them what to expect.

Before Randy could be put on the transplant list, a committee at the hospital had to review his test results and consider his case for approval. They met on Friday morning, after the transplant team had completed their tests. Based on the team's recommendation, the committee approved the transplant and sent an authorization request to his insurance company about noon. By three o'clock that afternoon the insurance company sent their approval and Randy was added to the heart transplant waiting list.

That is a miracle. Anyone who has ever traversed the bureaucratic red tape of a transplant board and getting the go-ahead for a transplant from an insurance company knows that just doesn't happen. But that wasn't much of a miracle compared to what happened next! At 6:00 p.m. that very night they were prepping him and getting him ready for surgery. They had already found a donor heart.

Debbie, Randy's wife, was trying to catch up on her work when she got his call, "Debbie, they just came in and told me that they found a donor heart." She didn't believe him. She thought they had given him some medication or something. Randy kept saying, "No, they've found a heart." And she said, "Well, I'll come up there as soon as I get off." And Randy said, "Debbie, there's a lady in here prepping me right now." Debbie rushed to the hospital, went to the nurses' desk, and said in disbelief, "Now, I'm not sure what's going on but Randy called and said that they've found a heart," and they said, "Yeah, we're getting him ready now."

A little after eleven o'clock, as family and friends were still gathering at the hospital, Randy was wheeled to surgery. By three o'clock the next morning, Randy was back in his room, his new heart in place. Talk about your life changing instantaneously! That's pretty fast, my friends!

Randy's recovery went so well the first week that he was scheduled to go home. Then on Friday during his walk he made a few less rounds than usual. When he passed the nurses station, he said, "I'm not feeling real good; I think I need to go lie down." So they helped him to his room. Instead of going home that evening as planned, he was whisked back to his room in CICU while the doctors tried to figure out what was going on.

While they were evaluating the situation, Randy's heart stopped beating. Debbie had just left his room when she heard one of the nurses call for a "Code Blue" over the intercom. When she looked down the hall, she could see into Randy's room, and what she saw no one should ever have to see. A nurse was on top of her husband, administering CPR. His heart started again as the room filled with hospital personnel. In less than an hour, it stopped again. They got him stabilized, but by Wednesday they took him back into surgery to open his chest so they could look at the heart. They didn't find anything abnormal and never learned why Randy's heart had quit beating twice.

In spite of all the drama, Randy's recovery then proceeded uneventfully. He had only a few bouts of minor rejection; that was nothing compared to what he saw others going through while he was on the heart-transplant floor. When he had a little rejection flare-up, they'd hook him up to an IV at home, run it for two or three days, and everything would be fine.

Much sooner than was expected, Randy was back at work, but his life never returned to normal: It got better! His family became closer. Two of his children still lived at home at the time, one in middle school and the other in high school. Randy became more sensitive to their needs and his need to have them nearby. This combination resulted in the Welch house's becoming the neighborhood hangout.

Randy said he couldn't leave his room most mornings without first putting on a bathrobe because he never knew how many kids had ended up spending the night. He'd find kids in the three extra bedrooms, on all three couches, and covering the living-room floor. And he loved having them there.

Randy says he never struggled with "empty nest syndrome" later in life. He was given the gift of being there for his children, and he has treasured seeing them grow up and fly the coop. And getting to know his five grandchildren—that has been priceless.

Randy also feels blessed to have opportunities he would not have had without his transplant. The kids who used to hang out at the house still stop by, even when they know Randy's now grown children aren't there, and Randy gets to mentor them. He sees every visit to the doctor's office as a chance to share God with somebody. Even the wheelchair he uses as a result of back problems has its advantages. "People who never would have acknowledged me stop to talk," Randy explained. "God uses everything. It doesn't matter what it is. There is no such thing as 'good' circumstances or 'bad' circumstances. If we allow Him to lead us through circumstances, then they're all good. I think the thing that the Lord really opened my eyes to is that there is no circumstance that He can't handle."

That last point is the one that gives Randy, and me, total peace.

Charles Keith Hawkes

Keith Hawkes read about my brain injury and the pending surgery, which had passed the scrutiny of the Ben Franklin approach, and he filled me in on his experience with brain shunts. I hope I never get as experienced as Keith, but I'm grateful that he told me his story. I love stories that have a good ending!

Keith was nineteen when he found out he had the same condition I have, hydrocephalus, pressure on the brain from excess spinal fluid. His brain shunt was installed, and it seemed to remedy the problem until one day eight years later when Keith lost consciousness. He was rushed into surgery where the doctors discovered that adhesions were blocking the flow of cerebrospinal fluid. They corrected the problem, and Keith enjoyed good health for the next twenty-two years.

Shunts normally last about fifteen years, but Keith's "miracle shunt" held up for thirty! Unfortunately, when it failed, the problems that accompanied replacing it were huge. Keith left work with a pounding headache on Friday of Labor Day weekend, 2006. By Saturday, he was comatose in the hospital and surgery was performed to replace the shunt. Almost immediately blood clots clogged up the new shunt, so a second shunt was installed. It, too, got blocked by blood clots, so a third shunt was installed. Three years have passed since that incident, and thus far the shunt is working as it should.

I wish that was all there is to the story, but Keith suffered severe brain injuries from the extreme pressure that built up during the prolonged time it took to get a shunt to function. After two months in the hospital he was moved to a rehab hospital where doctors told his family that Keith probably would not get better, so they suggested that Keith be moved to a nursing home.

Enter our heroine: Keith's wife, Sandra. Many people thought she was in serious denial about the hopelessness of Keith's condition, but Keith tells me that twenty years of marriage had shown him her unwavering faith. Sandra Hawkes was unwilling to have her husband "vegetating" in a nursing home the rest of his life. She enlisted the help of the nursing staff in the neurosurgery wing of Memorial Hermann Baptist Hospital to find Keith an alternative option to the nursing home. The Lord led them to one of the top rehabilitation hospitals in the world for people with brain and spinal-cord injuries, the Institute for Rehabilitation and Research in Houston, Texas.

Immediately, Keith began to have positive results. Within a week he started to wake up from his coma. It was obvious that he had brain damage, since he could not talk or walk. He started physical therapy and occupational therapy, and he went to the gym five days a week for intense workouts. His speech therapist exercised his brain daily with logic and deduction puzzles. Over time he relearned how to bathe, dress, and feed himself, and at the end of three months he was functioning normally. Keith Hawkes had embraced his struggle and was released to go home.

The rehabilitation process continued on an outpatient basis; and today while Sandra still helps Keith with home workouts, his recovery is more than remarkable—he knows it is miraculous. Recently, Keith's neurosurgeon told him that Keith's brain injuries were as bad as brain injuries can get, but that Keith's injuries had "completely healed." Keith chalks that diagnosis up to "prayer—praying without ceasing."

Keith had prepared in advance for his struggle. He had a fantastic support group in the members of his Sunday school class. They relieved Sandra at the hospital, and they read the Sunday school lessons and other books to him. They just talked to him as if he weren't in a coma, and he was able to recall a good portion of what had been said when he woke up.

Two special young men, Todd and Travis Stephenson, even gave up their Christmas Eve to play their guitars and sing Christmas and contemporary Christian music in Keith's hospital room. They kept Keith company during what could have been one of his loneliest, saddest days. Keith says what they did shows that no outreach is too small to offer someone who is suffering.

And just to prove my point one more time, I'm going to let Keith say it: "Although this seemed like a very dark time in my life, I'm kind of (in a strange way) glad that it happened (although I don't want to go through it again). It has truly been a blessing because it has brought me closer to the Lord. I'm working harder to live the life that God wants me to live. God is good!"

Finally, Keith says that Isaiah 38:1, which tells us to keep our house in order, has significant meaning to him, and he cautions me—and you—to do as the scripture says. Life really can, and often does, change in an instant.

Today

Right now as you are reading, you think you know what you're going to be doing when you put this book down. But you might get "the call" that someone you love is in trouble or has died, or you could have a stroke, an aneurism, or even a heart attack when you try to get out of bed. I really hope you don't. But the point is, we just don't know what might happen. And we need to live not in fear but in a constant state of preparedness.

It is possible to be a positive thinker and a realist. Realistically, I'm positive we're all going to die. Factually, some of us do go to sleep at night and just never wake up, but most of us are going to face some health challenges like the ones we've just read about before we get to "fly away to glory," as the chorus of one of my favorite songs states. When you hit the tough spots, be ready to engage your struggle. Face it, embrace it, overcome or accept it, whichever the need may be. Like me, you'll be amazed at how God uses your circumstances in a Romans 8:28 way!

10

Marriage Struggles

For those of you who have skipped over the previous nine chapters to read this one first, you are in good company! I fully expect this chapter to be the most well read because the highest percentage of this book's readership will relate to marriage struggles. If there are any marriages in which there have been no struggles, even minor ones, I am unaware of them.

Most of you know that I have the great fortune of being married to the Redhead. I'm not braggin', just stating the fact. It is no secret that I'm wild about her. I probably talk about that Redhead more than any other subject I speak on, and with good reason! She has been my personal cheerleader and my life for sixty-two wonderful years. She has given me the "home court advantage" since the day we got married. I'll tell folks that if she ever leaves me—I'm going with her!

I have to confess, I think I got a better deal than she did. Being married to the Redhead just hasn't been much of a struggle, but when she married me, I didn't know a thing about how to be a good husband. This will be a shock to most of you, but I actually believed that it was the Redhead's "duty" to wash my clothes, clean my house, and cook my meals . . . all three of them, every day!

Why I had this idea is a mystery to me. My father died when I was five years old. My mother never remarried, so I didn't get to see firsthand how married couples lived or what they did for one another. I hadn't learned that there is an art to compromise and that just believing something to be true doesn't make it so. It was about three weeks into my marriage when the Redhead taught me the truth about my "three home-cooked meals per day" fallacy. On the other two issues (laundry and cleaning) I must say she has always done more than her fair share of the work—okay, all of the work. But she assures me that she didn't mind one bit, especially after we hired a housekeeper to clean the house and wash our clothes.

I know some of you are wondering if the Redhead worked outside of our home. She did work off and on throughout our marriage. Most of the time it was in our own business, but she put in hours at our office when she still had four children living at home. She knows what it is to juggle work and family because she was doing that when my work took me out of town most days of the week. Now you're beginning to understand my fascination with the Redhead. She could, and did, do it all!

Seriously, the kinds of struggles we dealt with are, I believe, common to most newlyweds. When I started writing this chapter, I asked the Redhead what she thought our biggest struggle had been, and she said it was learning that you had to consider someone else's needs and wants. She said, "When two previously independent individuals say 'I do' and set up housekeeping, they arrive with their own ideas about how marriage works, who does what jobs; who pays the bills, earns the money, bathes the kids, etc. Learning how to compromise and becoming willing to do things that you might not enjoy, for the sake of your mate, takes some time. Overcoming selfishness is possibly the biggest struggle of all."

I wholeheartedly agree! When I learned to put the needs of the Redhead ahead of my own, I learned "the secret" to marital happiness. You have to *want* your mate to be happy, even at your expense. When your mate is happy, he or she will ultimately *want you* to be happy too. And it is nearly impossible to outgive each other when the motive is love.

The Redhead and I know many couples who have struggled mightily to save and prosper their marriages. We've prayed with and for couples who have dealt with addiction, adultery, pornography, anger, physical abuse, devastating financial difficulties, life-changing health issues, ill or disabled or special-needs children, mental illness, and more. If you can think of something that puts stress on a relationship, you've thought of something that has been the last straw for some marriages.

Yet we've seen marriages that seemed unsalvageable survive and thrive. We shake our heads in wonder at the goodness of God and what He has done in our own family with the marriage of our daughter Julie and her husband, Jim. I've written about their relationship in previous books, so I'll just briefly say that they separated after eleven difficult and often very unhappy years. With the support of their church fellowship, the counsel of their associate pastor, and the grace of God, they reunited after a little more than a year, and now their relationship is the envy of many who know them. They and their children are by far the biggest benefactors, but when a couple makes the choice to fight for the commitment they've made and do it together, miraculous, healing changes take place. The couples whose stories follow are wonderful examples of what happens when God becomes the focus in marital relationships.

Sharon and William Cothron

In the past several years the Redhead and I have had the pleasure of sharing many Thanksgiving meals with William and Sharon Cothron. Conversation is always lively and positive because they are both passionate people. They are passionate about the Lord and the full-time ministry He has called them to, Marriage Reconciliation. They have been blessed to see over 250 marriages restored since they set out to show distraught couples how God could and would heal their marriages if they let Him.

I'll tell Sharon's side of the story first and then William's. (There are always two sides to these "bad marriage" stories.)

Sharon

Sharon Cothron didn't know what she was doing wrong, but her choices caused her to suffer a lot of heartache and pain. She ran away from home at an early age and got married before she turned sixteen. A year later she had her first child, three years later her second child arrived, and after seven and a half years Sharon decided to divorce her husband. He wasn't making her happy anymore.

Very quickly after that divorce was final, Sharon found herself in another relationship and after a couple of months married her second—and thankfully still present—husband William. But that marriage was actually much worse than the first one! Sharon says it was a true case of "out of the frying pan and into the fire!" The marriage was horrible. They fought all the time. They were angry. They were each expecting the other one to "make" them happy.

After three years and another child Sharon didn't know where to go or what to do. She had exhausted her friends and parents with her constant complaining about the marriage. She had even worn herself out with her whining—and when William quit talking to her, she knew they were in serious trouble. They separated, and Sharon cried all the way from Florida back to Texas, with her three children gathered round her in the airplane.

But God used her brokenness to bring her to Him. Sharon had made a decision for Christ as an eleven-year-old and had been obedient in being baptized, but she did not understand, and was not taught, what lordship meant. She didn't know how to allow Jesus to take control and be the Lord of her life every day. She didn't know that was what she had been doing wrong.

Now, with nowhere else to turn, Sharon turned to Christ. She cried out, "Lord! I know there is something wrong within me. Show me what's wrong within me." And not in a voice but with great clarity the Lord impressed on her mind and heart the following: *My child, I have always loved you. No one has ever loved you like I do, and I created you for Me. But you've never cared what I wanted.*

Sharon says her heart broke then over how she had hurt Him. Always before, her tears had been for herself, but this time they were for the pain she had caused Jesus. She had been rebellious. Rebellious toward her parents, running away, not asking Him if she should marry, getting divorced, remarried, separated, all without even considering what God would want her to do. She said, "Lord, here's this huge mess. I don't know what to do with it. I don't have any answers; I don't have any plans; I don't have anything. I am willing to do whatever You tell me to do."

One step at a time the Lord started directing Sharon. William had said he never wanted to see Sharon again, but he called her and asked her to come home. Sharon told him she didn't know if she would, that she was trying to find out what God wanted her to do, and that she needed time to do that. William didn't understand what was going on, but he waited impatiently for her decision.

By the end of the week Sharon knew that she was to go home to William. God made it clear that William was not a changed man but that Sharon was a woman with a little seed of faith. She returned to Florida and faithfully studied the Bible for the next four months, asking the Lord to teach her what He wanted her to know and understand about Him. Then she began to attend a small church just a few miles from her home that embraced and loved her and her children.

The situation with William wasn't improving, but Sharon could tell he was watching her. In fact, the nicer she was to him, the angrier he got. At first Sharon tried to share some of the things that God was doing in her life, but that blew up in her face. A Christian brother showed her 1 Peter 3, about being submissive (God's way—not what man thinks), and Sharon realized that William would see Christ by seeing Christ in her changed life. She was to live her life for Christ. That was all she had to do. Be quiet, be respectful, have a gentle spirit, trust God, and just be a godly example. But Sharon screamed, "Lord, I don't know how to do that!" Sharon wasn't raised to be that kind of person. She couldn't even envision herself being able to live that way . . . it just seemed impossible! But then she'd find scriptures like, "With God all things are possible." Sharon knew she had to focus on Him, rely on Him, and trust Him. She didn't always do it perfectly, but every time she found herself on her knees, begging for forgiveness and asking for strength to keep going, she grew closer to the Lord.

Sharon never invited William to church. She never invited him to do anything spiritual with her. She entrusted him to the Lord, prayed for him, and asked God to use her as a godly example before him, but she never manipulated him. During that time William was working and being a provider, but he was not a real husband to Sharon. That is when God showed her Isaiah 54:5–17 and Sharon knew that with God she was complete. God became the joy of her life. Her misery was replaced with peace, and William saw the change taking place in her.

William

William's first marriage lasted only a year. When it was over, he was so distraught that he was considering suicide, and then he met Sharon in a bar. She had lost her job, so William decided to rescue her. They got married. They were two miserable people, and the marriage started off "just horrible."

First they tried moving to Arizona, then to Florida, but their problems always caught up with them. William was so self-centered, he didn't even know how miserable he was. Sharon knew she was miserable and didn't mind letting it show. William would come home, see the misery on her face, and ask, "If I go back outside and come back in, do you think you could possibly wipe some of that misery off of your face and be a little more joyous when you see me?" Somehow, that didn't help matters, and they separated.

William was miserable with her, but found out that he was more miserable without her, so he asked her to come back. When she did, he saw the total change in her. He saw her joy and her peace. One night when they went out to dinner, he asked her what she'd like to drink. She said, "Just a Coke." He said, "No, I mean, don't you want your favorite, rum and Coke?" She said, "No, I've decided I'm not going to drink anymore." William became furious. He wasn't going to live with a saint. He'd grown up Catholic, and he wasn't having any "saints" in his life. He told her he would divorce her if she didn't do what he said. But God had given Sharon a peace that He was her source and her provider and William couldn't deter that. When he told her he'd divorce her, Sharon said he was free to go. With that declaration, William had no power; manipulation and control were dead.

William accepted the new arrangement. In fact, he especially enjoyed the peace and quiet he got on Sundays when Sharon took the children to church. He could eat his hamburgers and french fries and watch his football in peace without kids running around screaming. It was quiet. Sharon didn't nag or pester him to go to church. She just faithfully took the children every Sunday.

Eventually, William picked up a Bible and read it. The first time he read it, he got angry. Then he started reading it again, and the Lord convicted him about going to church, so he asked Sharon if he could go to church with her. He went and listened, and she didn't say, "Well, what'd you think? Did you like the people? What was the message?" She just let William think for himself.

About two months later he told her he'd like to go with her again. When the preacher gave the invitation to accept Christ, William shocked Sharon by going to the front of the church and giving his life to Jesus. He was baptized that day, and his life has not been the same since. He knew he wanted Jesus to be Lord of his life, so he made two commitments: he would go to church regularly and he would give at least 10 percent of his income to the Lord.

Sharon and William

William became a Christian in 1973. In 1976 he and Sharon decided to go to Bible college. Their only motivation was to learn more about Jesus and take Bible classes. They never graduated, but while they were there, they found themselves ministering to couples who were struggling. It happened so many times that they asked the Lord, "Do you realize who we are? We're not capable of doing this!" And the Lord showed them that He is the One who equips them, who makes their counsel possible. William and Sharon realized that the Lord wanted to use them because of their testimony about what He had done in their marriage.

Through a series of events, the Cothrons have been coleaders of a Marriage Reconciliation class at Richland Hills Church of Christ, near Ft. Worth, Texas, since 1991, and they also counsel couples individually. They say the reason Christians divorce is "because we live in a culture of divorce, it is considered acceptable today." They say selfishness is the biggest problem they see—which proves once again that the Redhead *is* always right. And they say that they always start by telling couples, or the half of the couple who comes to the class, that they have to reconcile with God first. Jesus is the only One who can bring them peace, and if Jesus is the rock, the foundation the marriage is built on, the marriage will bring glory, honor, and praise to the Lord. It will also bring joy to the marriage relationship.

William says he and Sharon are one in ministry, in life, in finances, in all things. Jesus is the focus of their lives. Their marriage has been a testimony to their children and to couples across America, and now around the world as they travel to South Africa and China delivering the message God has charged to them. This couple has been a blessing in my life, and I am thrilled to share them and their story with you.

Linda and Gary Van Buren

The last time I heard the word *wow* expressed so convincingly was when I had the pleasure of being aboard a jet with a little girl who was on her first flight. She stepped into the first-class cabin, stopped, looked around, and with big eyes filled with wonder and a voice full of awe said, "Wow!" Linda Van Buren, in an email of encouragement to me, recently said exactly the same thing, in exactly the same way, except she and her husband Gary used the word "Wow!" to describe the transformation that has taken place in their marriage.

Wow wasn't the word Linda was using in 1998. She was actually referring to her marriage as *it* at the time. She knew there was something wrong with *it*, but she didn't know what *it* was, or how to fix *it*. She knew there were no perfect marriages, and after eighteen years her marriage more than fit the "not perfect" category.

That's about the time Linda purchased my cassette tape/CD series called "Courtship After Marriage." She had used other books and programs of mine to help her in her business life. Surely, she thought, if she could apply what she would learn in "Courtship After Marriage," if she could just change herself enough, everything would fall into place.

Linda told me, "That is good in theory, but if someone has no desire or, for that matter, sees nothing that needs changing, then it is hopeless." And that is just where their relationship stood after both she and Gary listened. Linda put the tape series on the bookshelf, where it gathered dust, just like their marriage.

By 2001 Linda felt like she and Gary had hit rock bottom. Gary was spending lots of time away from the house, and when he was home, he wasn't happy. They scheduled a cruise, and Linda held on to the hope that the cruise might possibly rekindle their love. They did have a great time, but when they got home, everything returned to status quo.

Several weeks after the cruise Linda was crushed to discover that she was not the only woman in her husband's life. Gary apologized. He wanted to fix it—to make everything right again. Linda said, "There were so many tears; no fighting, just an incredibly hurt spirit." That same week Linda's minister and his wife stopped by the house and were still talking when Gary got home from playing golf. Linda says that Gary had not been a "God guy" before, but that night they all prayed together, and God moved into their house.

Soon, Gary noticed all the books on Linda's bookshelf about how to repair your relationships, improve your marriage, etc. Then he came across the Courtship After Marriage series and said, "You were trying all along, and I wouldn't see it." Gary's realization and his admission to Linda reduced both of them to tears. Gary asked Linda if he could put the tapes in his car, and he began to listen to them on his commute to work. He arrived home one day and told Linda he was amazed to discover that *it* (marriage) is all about honor. He said, "If you honor your spouse—that person returns it tenfold!"

One of the ways Gary began to honor Linda was by bringing home little gifts. Linda loves the story Gary tells about the day he saw a small bouquet of flowers next to the checkout counter where he was paying for gas. When he picked the flowers up to pay for them, the man behind him said, "What did you do wrong that you are buying her flowers? Don't buy her those! You should buy her roses!" Gary said, "I didn't do anything wrong. I just want her to know I'm thinking about her." The girl who ran the cash register heartily agreed with Gary.

Today Linda has a whole vase full of little Mylar balloons to remind her of the many times Gary has gone out of his way to let her know he cherishes her. It doesn't have to be roses or diamonds; it is the simple act of letting your partner know he or she is in your thoughts that counts. The quote of mine Gary says he shares a lot is this: "It is all about honor. Women, treat your husbands like you would your hairdressers. And men, treat your wives like you would a person asking for directions." Linda says, "Gary lives by that quote. Even when I slip—he never does. *Never!*"

Linda, too, has made big changes. She credits Gary's desire to identify the problem, take action, and change with her willingness to be more loving and to give back more than she had before. They both say their relationship is "something to behold." Their kids love being around them, and they hope their marriage is an inspiration to their children and their spouses.

But I believe the most inspiring part of Linda and Gary's story was revealed in their email giving us permission to include their story in *Embrace the Struggle*. Julie had written Linda, saying that she didn't know how private they were about the struggle they had survived in their marriage, or if they ministered to other couples, but that we'd like them to pray about allowing us to use their story in this book. In Linda's reply she wrote, "If what happened to us (which is not un-usual in today's times—unfortunately) and the positive end result (which *is* more unusual—unfortunately) would be a source of inspi-ration to someone else, then we are all for that.

"We are not real concerned about other people's perceptions about infidelity. Our friends know and have always supported our decision. Our children know, and they celebrate the strength of our marriage. We have told them that God moved in our lives and helped us create the changes we made to restore our relationship.

"The ministry we do is by example. It is not focused on 'here's what happened,' but we set an example of a strong, loving mar-riage."

I wish more couples who have survived the agonizing wounds of adultery were as willing as Linda and Gary are to be transparent about how God has healed their marriage. They are what I call "available and obedient to God." They have not been led to lead a marriage reconciliation ministry like William and Sharon Cothron, but when asked to share their marriage experience, strength, and hope, they did. I believe Linda and Gary's openness and honesty will influence many couples to make positive changes in their marriages.

The Truth

It is my concern that the majority of marriages consist of two people "existing" together, as Linda and Gary Van Buren were. Neglect, frustration, hopelessness, and the inability to communicate all lead to disaster in marriage. I want to point out that the adultery the Van Burens had to deal with was a symptom of the apathy they had about their marriage. If you've thought to yourself, *Surely, there is more to marriage than this*, or *I guess I can accept this, make do, and get by with things the way they are*, or *I think I can last until the kids turn eighteen or leave for college*, your marriage needs to be shaken up, stirred up, and reconfigured. God wants so much more for us! It is a disgrace to Him when we "settle" for anything less than the kind of marriage that will glorify and honor Him.

In some ways volatile relationships like the one Sharon and William Cothron had have a better chance of surviving than "smoldering" ones. At least it is obvious to everyone that there is a problem. If you can't say that the relationship you have with your spouse is the most intimate, most important, most fun and joyous relationship you have, then, my friend, you are in the midst of a marriage struggle, and I challenge you to embrace that struggle and change your life and the life of your spouse for the better!

If you do, one day you might just get to have a relationship with someone you love as much as I love that Redhead of mine. And that's better than good!

11

My Family's Struggle
with My Struggle

Seldom do people struggle alone. They may feel lonely at times, but in most cases there are people helping, supporting, praying, or coming alongside those who are facing challenges. Possibly, I have chosen the wrong title for this chapter. There are many who would take exception to my implying that helping the one they love is a struggle, because there is nothing they would do otherwise. They want to help, they want to serve, and they're happy to be of assistance. But everyone knows that there is a huge difference between helping someone for six to eight weeks while a broken wrist heals and helping someone with a chronic condition that appears to be without end. It isn't that anyone minds helping a loved one or friend, but it can be a struggle—or make that a "juggle"—in the lives of those who step up to help.

The Redhead

Short-term situations are trying enough. But how can we possibly convey our gratitude for the ones who endlessly take care of our needs when we can't? Personally, I am grateful beyond words for the family I have. The Redhead sees to so many things now that I used to do for myself. For instance, short-term-memory loss plays havoc with medications. I happen to be a believer in nutritional supplements. I've been taking pills, capsules, power drinks, and extra vitamins since the early 1950s. I only take a few medications, but the supplements I consume increase the number of pills I take to, well, excess. I never minded counting all those pills and setting up my morning and evening doses. And I'm grateful the Redhead is a good sport about my nutritional hobby. Without her help, no telling how many pills I would or wouldn't take.

The Redhead also makes sure I take care of my business obligations. These days we go everywhere together—and that is quite a change from her being alone several days a week while I traveled across the country. She assures me that she doesn't mind our new routine, and I know I would feel the same if the situation were reversed, but I want to be sure she stays in contact with her friends and that she gets a chance to socialize apart from me as well. I have to admit, though, I sure do miss her while she is out!

The Whole Team

Our children either come en masse, or take turns going with the Redhead and me to doctor's appointments. They like to "get the scoop" for themselves, and they know for a fact I won't remember what the doctor said. They give us rides if we're going to be out after dark, and if either one of their parents lands in the hospital, immediate plans are made for around-the-clock surveillance! We're glad we were nice to our children when they were little. It's really paying off!

My change in work habits has impacted everyone in our family on some level. As I said, the Redhead makes every trip with me now. Julie also. Tom has had to rearrange many of our affairs at the office, which has impacted Cindy and my granddaughter Katherine, not to mention the entire staff, and especially my executive assistant of more than thirty years, Laurie Magers. Thankfully, we all understand that we can only deal with what is in front of us today. Tomorrow we will face tomorrow. Waiting to see how well I recover from my brain-shunt surgery does leave some things up in the air, so what are we to do? We're embracing the struggle together!

The Ziglars Speak

I believe the best way for you to know what it has been like for my family to embrace the struggle with my brain injury is to let them have the floor and speak for themselves. If you wonder why the Redhead hasn't contributed to this chapter personally, it's because when I asked her if she would, she laughed and said this book wasn't long enough for her to say all she wanted to say on the subject of embracing the struggle . . . if the struggle we were talking about in this chapter was me! She's had sixty-two consecutive years of embracing me, and she wants more than a few paragraphs to tell about it. So she's going to tell it all in a book called *The Redhead Speaks*. No, I don't feel afraid. I trust her. And I know there won't be any arguments about the particulars of any of the stories she tells because I won't be able to remember if she's right or wrong. It's a good thing I trust her!

At my request, my children and one of my granddaughters have written about how my fall has changed their lives and what they struggle with. It is difficult to hear how my family hurts, but it also fills my heart with gratitude for the way they love and cherish me. You'll hear from my daughter Julie first, then Cindy and Tom, then my granddaughter Katherine Lemons.

Julie

My biggest struggle with Dad's fall happened within the first forty-eight hours after the accident. The night Dad fell comes to mind in vivid chunks of memory. Almost like paintball splats, they assault my mind. Bam! The phone rings too late at night. Bam! Mom's voice, strained and fearful, "Your father has taken a fall down the stairs. He hit his head." Oh no! Bam! "The ambulance is taking him to the hospital."

For an hour and twenty minutes I raced toward Plano, Texas. It was midnight when I burst into the emergency waiting room. I wanted to yell ahead, across the lobby, "Where is my dad, Zig Ziglar?" Instead, I forced myself to slow to a walk, and I measured my words so I wouldn't cry. The receptionist pushed a button and pointed toward the automatic doors that swished open in answer to my question. I was drawn down the sterile hall, away from all that had been, toward the unknown and into a world of faith ever expanding.

I soon found my mother—on a gurney in the hallway! What was going on? She was being checked out by doctors too! She had gone white and cold and clammy. Her arm hurt; her heartbeat was irregular. My mother, who had had a heart attack almost two years earlier and received an arterial stent as well, looked as if she were about to have another one. "I think it's just the stress of all this," she said reassuringly, as she patted my hand. Oh me!

"Where is Daddy?" I asked. Mom pointed toward a corner room

and told me Cindy was with him and that we were waiting for some test results but that Dad would be kept for observation at the very least. I left Mom with a friend who had rushed to the hospital to be with Mom and Dad until family could arrive and went to check on Dad.

When I walked in, Daddy was subdued. He was too quiet. He said hello and kissed me, but he didn't joke about dragging us out in the middle of the night like he had some months earlier when he'd had a glaucoma attack. His head was scraped and he was uncomfortable and cold on the too-narrow table they called a bed. Cindy filled me in on what had been happening since she arrived and left to be with Mom. Thankfully, there were no broken bones, but we were still waiting for the CT scan results. At the least, Dad had a serious concussion.

"Where's your mother?" Dad asked. Wow! That was a loaded question. I wondered if anyone had told Dad what Mom was up to. Fortunately, a nurse was just pushing Mom into Dad's room on her "bed," so I didn't have to explain. Then there we were with Dad on one side of the room and Mom on the other. Cindy and I stood between them, confounded and stricken with the reality that life does turn on a dime. Both of our parents were being held for overnight observation. Tom was still out of town. What a mess. And that's how it all started. That is how the struggle began.

The next morning Mom's heartbeat had settled back into a regular rhythm. After she had a chance to calm down, it returned to normal on its own. Dad's CT scan results, however, showed two brain bleeds, so he had to be checked into the hospital where he could be examined frequently for potential brain swelling. We were told we'd hope for the best but that sometimes brain bleeds could turn into a bad deal.

The struggle felt so intense. Dr. Robert Atkins, of the Atkins Diet fame, kept coming to mind. He had died almost four years earlier of a head injury he sustained when he slipped on icy pavement and hit his head. My father's very life was on the line. We prayed and waited.

Dad had his first dizzy spell within twelve hours of the fall, and we were told that wasn't uncommon. We knew from an experience I had with a concussion that asking the same questions over and over after a hard hit on the head was normal, so we were not overly concerned when Dad began to repeat himself. We figured it would clear up in three or four days like it did with my concussion, but it didn't.

Everything wasn't all right, but Daddy wasn't going to die. The worst part of the struggle was over for me. Daddy was alive and that was a good starting place! All that was left was to see how God would use Dad's circumstances to His glory, and I'm often speechless at what God has done and is doing in Dad's life and mine.

As his editor, I struggle with Dad's writing. More and more of it has fallen to me (I'm some of what Dad calls the "very good help" he has, along with his executive assistant, Laurie Magers). He still dictates information and talks endlessly about what we can put in the book and which book he's going to write next. He has so many books and so much material that he started long before his fall, but it is now entirely up to me to organize what he has written. I know he trusts me to be true to how he would handle everything, but at times the magnitude of that responsibility washes over me in a huge wave of doubt. I just want to honor him and to honor God with Dad's writing. I am grateful beyond measure for the fifteen years of preparation Dad and I have both had for this time in our lives. I just remember God really is in control and then I'm okay again.

Can you imagine going from the privacy of your little home office, where you sit in front of a computer and quietly edit books all day, to going on stage with fireworks exploding all around and seeing and hearing eighteen thousand cheering, clapping, foot-stomping Zig

Ziglar fans jump to their feet to welcome your father? I couldn't either. But God could and did, and He prepared me and Dad well in advance for that very moment.

In all of my life I never wanted or expected to be before any audience, but when Dad needed me, I knew it would be okay. I cherish the time I am on stage interviewing Dad, and I cherish meeting the people who tell him their lives are better because of his influence. (You've read the stories of many of those people in this very book.) Seeing my father through the eyes of others has only heightened my love, respect, and admiration for him. He was already my hero. I'm awed by the number of people who tell me they consider him their surrogate father and their hero. Dad is such a humble man; if I had never traveled with him, I would not know how deeply special he is to so many.

Cindy

When Dad fell down the stairs on the evening of March 7, 2007, little did I know that my life would be changed forever. Dad had made one of his legendary speeches on that very day. It would be his last. He had suffered a brain injury when he fell. I had an inkling of how his life might change since I had volunteered at an outpatient clinic for brain-injured people for several years with my therapy dog. The possibilities were overwhelming to me, and I slipped in and out of denial.

To see such a vibrant, energetic man change overnight was tragic for me. But as Dad recovered from his fall, I saw God begin to work in amazing ways. Dad could no longer make speeches the way he had, but he could make them with my sister Julie's help in an interview format. I was there for the first speech and was amazed at my sister's courage and strength as she guided our father in front of thousands of people.

There were mixed reviews afterward. Zig Ziglar was not the same Zig Ziglar that people had admired and loved for so many years. This Zig needed help from his daughter. She has, indeed, led him down an amazing path that touches and changes people's lives in ways we never dreamed of. I have witnessed standing ovations when Julie told the audience that Dad was living life on life's terms. It was so obvious that people needed to hear that. Transparency seemed to be a new motto for our family. A new journey had begun.

I have been all over the map with my emotions for Dad during these two years. I no longer have the father I have had for most of my fifty-six years. I am grieving the loss of that father. I now have a father who needs help and direction but still has his quick wit and intelligence and is more loving than ever. He has become sweeter, if that's possible, and filled with gratitude that most of us will never experience in our lifetimes. He is living the way he has taught other people to live—he is walking the walk in a way that is so precious it brings tears to my eyes every time I think of him. I don't want people to pity him, and I worry about his dignity. God is showing me how to let go of so many things. This is truly a time to give it all to Him.

I lose a little of my father every time I see him. He has good days and bad days. Sometimes I am filled with hope and encouraged when I see my "Old Daddy," the way he used to be. There are glimpses of that dad, and sometimes it seems almost cruel for I am reminded of what I have lost. Yet I try to be grateful for those glimpses because I know they are precious and a gift. I miss my daddy so much. I miss his "airport calls" and his "just because" calls. He has always called his children every day, and now that has pretty much stopped. When I do get one of his rare calls, I hang on to every word and try to memorize it, breathe it into my very soul, and hold it there forever, for I know the calls will stop completely one day. Every moment with Daddy is a treasure these days. It is unbearable to think about the future, so I try to stay in today. It's even more difficult to think about the past and what was.

This truly is a struggle, and embracing it on a daily basis makes me so weary. So I hunker down, keep my eyes on Dad's hero—Jesus—and try to be grateful for everything. We are to praise God for all of it, and sometimes it is so hard to do that. But when I do, I am reminded of how I am the most blessed girl in the universe to have such a precious father. Thank you, Jesus, thank you.

Tom

There is something about a true life struggle that makes you decide what is really important. Dad and I have had a great relationship for years—a relationship I believe most people would envy. When he fell and it became apparent that life was much tougher for him than it had ever been, I suddenly had to deal with all kinds of emotions.

I remember as a young man bragging to others that my dad could speak more than thirty hours with just an outline and not repeat himself! Not only that, but he could go eight hours, full speed ahead in front of a group and do it better and with more energy than anybody in the world could. Of course, as the years added up he couldn't go as long, but, still, even at eighty years old he could make everyone in the room believe he wasn't a day over sixty. That all changed when he fell. Now when he speaks in front of a group, it's not uncommon for him to repeat himself in the span of a few minutes.

When this first started happening, I was very self-conscious—*what will others think?* I thought. I then started really watching Dad and the audience, and I learned something incredible. Because we made no effort to hide the effects of his fall from the audience and were totally transparent about it, the people loved him even more and responded in even greater ways.

One particular event stands out in my mind. Over a period of two days Dad told the same story about Mom to this group of people five times. Every time was just a little different, but to me it was the same story . . . and inside it was tearing me up. The next day one of the seminar attendees came to me and said that he had brought to the event a friend who was having serious problems with his marriage. And after the *fifth* time Dad had told the same story, it finally got through to his friend: his friend broke down and started crying, ready to address his issue with his wife!

This was a real turning point for me and helped me understand what true transparency is. Dad for many years has prayed and asked God to use him, any way He saw fit, to further His kingdom. Of course, I thought God was using Dad's ability to win others over. Now I know that God is using his availability, not his ability. After all, if it was only ability, how could God get any credit? True transparency is when you are such a weak vessel, so transparent, that people see right through you to the One who created you. When people see Dad now and hear him tell stories, it's clear to everyone that the stories are not quite as eloquent as they used to be, but somehow they are even more powerful and more life-changing than they have ever been. That's because the power in what he is saying is not his own, and now everyone knows it.

Now when I am with Dad, I don't have that angst anymore. It's okay when he tells the same story. I know that God is arranging things I can't see, and someone I don't know is going to be impacted in a way I don't understand. As I was trying to understand all of this, I found a Bible passage that describes it perfectly, 2 Corinthians 12:9–10, "He [Christ] said to me, 'My grace is sufficient for you, for my power is made perfect in weakness. Therefore I will boast all the more gladly of my weaknesses, so that Christ's power may rest on me. That is why for Christ's sake I delight in weaknesses, in insults, in hardships, in persecutions, in difficulties. For when I am weak, then I am strong'" (NIV).

I especially like the last phrase, "For when I am weak, then I am strong." Now I know it's not only okay to be weak, it's a good thing!

Katherine

I have a very clear mental picture of the grandfather of my childhood. He is in his walking gear—khaki shorts, golf shirt (tucked in), white knee-high athletic socks, and those classic gray New Balance running shoes (before they were vintage). His gold-framed glasses sit squarely on his sun-bronzed nose, colored from years of walking and golfing under the intense Texas sun. His hair is black with strands of gray and always neatly combed. But his energy and excitement—those two things made the most indelible impression on my young mind. Whether he was running from one end of a stage to another or chasing after us grandchildren trying to eradicate a serious case of the goulirooshers (true story, and, yes, it's a real affliction in those under age ten), he was always on the move.

As a young child, one cannot yet imagine the effects of age, the way the years wear away at the memory and decrease physical strength. So it's difficult to think back to those days where I used to ride atop Granddaddy's shoulders, hunting for golf balls. I see him now, quieter, a little stooped over, and instead I have now become the strong one, the one guiding him. This transition, this struggle, is difficult to embrace.

I have always looked to my grandparents as the epitome of the perfect couple. I admire their love for each other; the way Mammaw speaks about Granddaddy when he isn't there or the way he looks at her from across a crowded table. These are the words and the glances that reflect a lifetime of love, devotion, and admiration. So it was no surprise when I married Chad Lemons in September, 2007, that I wanted these same qualities for our relationship. It was about this time when the effects of my grandfather's head injury began to worsen. I watched as my grandmother's companion of more than sixty years began to fade away a little more each week. Having just found this companionship for myself, I grieved for her, for her loss of the husband she had known for so many years. But I also grieved for me—the invincible man with the sun-bronzed skin and indomitable energy has become quieter, softer, more forgetful, and physically weaker.

As the weeks have progressed, I have watched as His wisdom has brought Granddaddy's struggle into perspective. A sudden fall and a head injury may have taken my grandfather's short-term memory, but it has not, and cannot, take away his faith in Christ or the love he has for his family. He has been stripped down to his very core, and what remains are faith and love; there is no room for superficial fillers but only the things that matter most.

My grandfather has always said that you gather your fruit for the mountaintop while in the valley; in other words, God allows us to endure struggles so that we are prepared for what He has for us ahead. It feels as though as a family we are gathering our fruit, embracing this struggle, and preparing for what God has for us in the future.

12

Spiritual Struggles

The most fascinating part of life is the spiritual aspect. I know there are those who say they don't believe there is a God of any kind, and there are those who are just not sure what they believe. If you fall into either category, I challenge you to consider that you've had a spiritual struggle to arrive at what you presently say you believe.

The biggest spiritual struggles I see typically involve admitting "there is a God, and it isn't me." I wish I knew who coined that phrase so I could give credit. That statement is so much more than clever. In chapter 3 I wrote about the day I accepted Jesus Christ as my Lord and Savior, but I didn't tell you what my spiritual condition had been up until that point. I had been brought up in the church, Baptist to be exact. My mother made sure all of us were there every time the doors opened. When I reached the age (usually between eight and twelve) when most children "make a decision" or choose to make it known by a public profession of faith that they believe in Jesus, I did what I felt was expected of me, and I was baptized.

Then, without any more thought or consideration, I went on living my life my way. Sure, I'd take the Redhead and my children to church every now and then. But I was careful to always have a pen and some paper with me so I wouldn't entirely waste my time while I was there. I could plan my schedule for the week, set goals—the to-do list possibilities were endless! The thought that I might learn something that could benefit me never occurred to me. The concept of meeting God there, well, that wasn't one of my expectations. I just didn't put any thought into God. I had too many other things to do. I was, after all, a man busy trying to provide for my family.

I pursued my goals, planned to increase my business, continued to give speeches every chance I got, and dreamed of the future. The closest thing to a spiritual experience I had was when I won a sales contest. I had to enjoy that feeling of being on top fast because the next sales contest would be underway on Monday and I'd have to get busy proving myself all over again.

I worked hard, so I was rewarded. But I always wanted more. I'd get to what I thought was the top and could see that I still had a long way to go. I was never content, never satisfied, never at peace. I thought I was just extremely motivated when I was actually spiritually bankrupt. If I had too much quiet time, I'd get uneasy. I felt like I should be doing something, staying busy, making life happen.

Then I met Sister Jessie, and she told me Jesus had been waiting on me a long time. She said I shouldn't make Him wait any longer, and she told me who He was and why I needed Him, over and over and over again. I finally heard with my heart what she had been telling me, and I surrendered my life to Him.

From that day forward my life has not been any of my business.

I began then to live for Christ, to honor Him, and He became my first thought, my first consideration, and my great joy. Through Him I am able to love that Redhead like I had never loved her before. My children, my associates, my friends, everyone I have contact with is someone God has put in my life, and I love them because of Him. I love them through Him.

I honestly don't worry about anything—ever. I know God is in control, and He has a purpose and direction for my life. All I have to do is the next right thing, and I do that by being available and obedient to do what He puts in front of me to do. Do I hear an audible voice? No. But the Holy Spirit prompts my heart into knowing what God would have me do. Then it is my responsibility to follow through on those promptings. I am always blessed when I am obedient, and it is my joy to serve Him.

Kristena Smith-Rivera

Kristena Smith-Rivera, whose motto is "Everything happens for a reason," had encouraging words for me about the "speed bump" God allowed in my life when I fell down the stairs. Her words highlight what I've been saying. She said, "Over the last two years I have 'let go and let God!' I have never been so *present* and in the moment as I have once I gave God the lead. I feel 2008 has almost been in slow motion as I have been focused and paying attention to each path God is leading me down. I can hardly wait to jump out of bed each day to see what He has in store for me. The most exciting paths are the ones with the struggles, as so many lessons and opportunities have been presented to me at each speed bump God has prepared for me."

When you quit struggling and "let go and let God" like Kristena has, you'll experience the same excitement about each new day that she has. With her attitude of complete trust in God, she may have struggles, but they aren't going to get the best of her. She has exercised her faith enough to know that the struggles just make her stronger. Try seeing challenges that come your way as opportunities to exercise your faith!

Owen Arnold

The most exciting paths really are the ones with the struggles. Cheryl Bierley wrote to say that she was asking God to give me all the strength and the faith I needed to fix my eyes on Him as I recovered and to tell me how her father ultimately ended up with the same brain-shunt surgery I had. Her story proves that what appears to be a physical struggle might actually be a spiritual one.

On October 5, 1996, Cheryl's father, Owen Arnold, suddenly had a totally unexpected and severe brain bleed. He was driving and blacked out when it happened, but by the grace of God he was able to call his wife Barb and let her know his location so she could call for help.

His last words over the phone to Barb were, "I'm fine, I just chipped a tooth." Fifty-four-year-old Owen Arnold then slipped into a coma that was to last six weeks. He had been completely healthy and strong up until that day. The doctors soon discovered that Owen had been born with a very rare and progressive disorder called Moyamoya syndrome, which affects arteries and capillaries and the routing of blood and can result in massive brain hemorrhages.

Owen was kept alive totally by machines and was not expected to live. He didn't have a personal relationship with God, but his family did, and they called on Him often those six long weeks. They and their church family prayed relentlessly for Owen and pled with God to spare his physical life so that he would have the chance to accept God's gift of eternal life. The miracle they experienced was twofold. Owen Arnold did wake up. Slowly he learned to breathe, eat, walk, and talk again. But even greater than the physical miracle was that he remembered his family's praying over his bedside. He also specifically recalled his pastor's sharing God's plan of salvation. When he could speak again, Owen confessed with his mouth that he accepted Christ as his Lord! Praise God!

Cheryl told me that her dad went home to be with the Lord in 2001 due to another, more severe bleed and they miss him terribly. But they are thankful because they know that with his spiritual battle won, his body and mind are now whole, and they will see him again someday!

DeDe Galindo

Our oldest granddaughter, DeDe Galindo, recently had a firsthand experience with a spiritual struggle for her beloved husband, Gus. She was telling me about how Gus had first noticed a mass under his rib cage. He immediately went to the doctor and was told he had a two-centimeter hematoma, a bad bruise, and that the lump would eventually go away. Several months later DeDe was hugging her husband and was alarmed to feel the lump, four times its original size. This time the doctor said it needed to come out and there was a possibility that it could be cancer.

The "internet doctor" came out in DeDe, and what she found during her hours and hours of searching scared and overwhelmed her. Abdominal sarcomas, if removed when they are two centimeters or less, are almost never fatal. If they are eight centimeters or over, there is an 80 percent chance of recurrence and the prognosis at that point is very poor. She kept the information to herself and hoped for the best.

DeDe said she had already been waiting longer than she thought it ought to take when Gus's surgeon appeared in the hospital waiting room and called her over to a more private area to talk about the surgery. She tells me that when the surgeon said, "It's a sarcoma, a little over eight centimeters in size," her world stopped. Nothing made sense to her anymore. She cried and sobbed and cried some more. Then she cried out to God with questions: Why did her sweet, wonderful, caring husband have cancer? What was she to do? How was she to cope and be strong for him and be strong for the kids? How could she ever live without the love of her life? Suddenly everything took on a new importance.

Step by step, day by day, DeDe relied on her faith. She believed that God was in control but wondered what God was doing. She had fear, but not fear that it wouldn't be okay in the end. Her fear was of the journey, the fear that comes when you don't know or understand the plan. But she did not let her fear take control, because DeDe knows that living in fear is not living in faith.

She believes that God never leaves us to struggle alone. She knew she had to trust Him, and in the end DeDe learned that she could do whatever she needed to do to take care of her husband, her four children, her work, and herself. DeDe is a Realtor, and she actually sold more real estate while Gus had cancer than she had in all the previous years. She learned that God really doesn't give us more than we can handle and that He gives us the power we need to face our circumstances.

DeDe's faith that God meant what He said through the apostle Paul in Romans 8:28 was confirmed as she saw her and her husband's relationships with God deepen. Through the radiation and chemo, they trusted Him. Through the dark times and the hard times, they trusted Him. Even when a CT scan, six months into Gus's treatments, revealed that the mass had returned in exactly the same location, they trusted Him. Needle biopsies of the mass were positive. The sarcoma had to be removed, and Gus underwent the same, difficult surgical procedure once again. The surgeon told DeDe that he removed not one but two sarcomas and that biopsies of both tumors were being sent to the lab. He told her that with the positive results of the needle biopsy and the fact that Gus's tumors looked like every cancerous sarcoma he'd ever removed, the news was not looking good.

A few weeks later DeDe and Gus went to the surgeon's office to review the biopsy results and find out what was next. The surgeon started the conversation by saying, "I don't understand what happened, but the biopsies on both tumors came back negative for sarcoma. I've ordered the needle biopsy and the surgical biopsies on both tumors to be done again." DeDe declared that she knew exactly what had happened! The doctor was seeing answered prayer. Jesus healed Gus.

DeDe believes in miracles. She has seen small ones throughout her life, and she feels blessed that God chose to heal Gus in such a dramatic and profound way that she "knows" and Gus "knows" and everybody who knew about Gus's struggle "knows" they have been given a miracle. She tells me she can relax because she knows Gus is not in remission, but that he is healed. She says through her spiritual struggle she grew stronger, more faithful, more self-assured, and more in love with Jesus. Today DeDe knows that "the journey *is* what we must experience to grow closer to *Him.*"

About that retest the unbelieving doctor requested, the needle biopsy was *still positive,* and the biopsies of the tumors were *still negative* for sarcoma, just like DeDe knew they would be.

Bill Blain

I am fortunate to know Bill Blain because I had the blessing of seeing him overcome one of the biggest physical and spiritual struggles a young man can face. I came to know Bill through his wife, Tangela, who was our company CPA for many years. They are a precious, fun couple whose lives are beautiful examples of what it is to live for Christ.

Have you ever committed yourself to a path and been convinced that the Lord was leading you in that effort only to have the path come to an abrupt end? When it happened, did you feel confused, abandoned, and even lost, without any hope? Bill experienced a traumatic medical event that instantly changed all he thought God was calling him to be. What follows is the story of his spiritual struggle and his spiritual victory.

Bill finished high school and immediately enlisted in the U.S. Navy as a jet mechanic. When he began serving his three-year tour of duty, Bill was an angry young man. But some of the navy chaplains got through to Bill's heart and turned him toward God and away from trouble.

When Bill's tour was up, he started looking for a job where he could make some "real money." And he found more than he was looking for. He got the job, and at about the same time he met Tangela! She was "swept away" by his blue eyes, and they were married after a very short courtship.

Bill was recovering from an injury he sustained on his job (he made a full recovery), when his pastor invited him to go to a "district" church function. At the meeting, when Brother J. W. Farmer made an impassioned plea to "serve God," Bill was deeply moved. On the way home he told his pastor he'd like to sign up to be the youth pastor. Over the next few months Bill's desire to serve God grew and simmered into his love for the navy. Soon it became clear that Bill's general call to serve had sharpened into a desire to become a navy chaplain.

When Bill looked into becoming a navy chaplain, he discovered he'd have to get a college degree and then finish seminary, and that was a pretty daunting task. But Tangela's new job put him in a position to go to the college he wanted to attend, and it put him close to the seminary he liked. It seemed as though everything was lining up with God's will, so Bill became a full-time student and Tangela brought home all the bacon.

Bill stayed in the reserves and was able to put in his two weeks in the summer and his "weekend warrior" time while he was in college. When he began seminary, he joined the Chaplain Candidacy Program, which allowed Bill to find out if he really wanted to serve as a chaplain for the Department of Defense. It also gave the branch of the service he wanted to serve in an opportunity to interview him and see if he'd be a good fit for them.

Bill was thrilled with his first set of orders. They sent him to minister to the air community—he loved to fly. As a chaplain who was going to be getting into airplanes, Bill was required to take flight physicals. He was always in excellent shape—until the day the doctor said, "Hey, we need to do another EKG. Something came up on your heart." Bill said, "Aw, you guys . . . your machine is broken!"

After another EKG and an examination by a cardiologist, Bill was told he had Wolff-Parkinson-White syndrome, a condition that can lead to life-threatening arrhythmia. When Bill found out he was grounded from flying because of the condition, he also found out there was a surgical procedure that could correct the problem. Without a second thought he said, "Let's fix it!"

All his life Bill Blain had been a hard charger. He depended on his strengths, his physical abilities, and his speaking abilities, to meet any challenge. He always knew he could do it! And that's the same attitude he took into the navy and that he was taking into surgery. Tangela didn't want him to have the surgery, but she knew Bill wasn't going to back down. Her mother made the trip to Dallas to take care of their children, and Tangela made the trip to be with Bill when he had the surgery.

Tangela kissed Bill good-bye and began the hour and forty-five minute wait. Three and a half hours and twenty-three shocks to his heart later, Bill Blain flatlined. His heart couldn't take the shocks that were designed to get it beating correctly, and it just stopped beating. Bill was dead.

Thankfully, the doctors were able to bring Bill back to life. When he woke up, he felt "really, really heavy," especially on his left side. Tangela could tell something wasn't right, and when Bill was finally able to explain how he felt, the nurse said, "Well, Chaplain, you've had a lot of anesthesia and you gave us a lot of trouble in the surgery room. This will wear off."

It didn't wear off. Bill had suffered a "cardiovascular accident." A blood clot had gone to the deepest part of his brain, and he'd had a stroke. There was nothing to be done except to survive it. As with all serious strokes, the exact degree of damage became apparent over the next several hours. Bill couldn't move his left arm or leg, and the left side of his face began to droop as the sensation of heaviness increased. He felt like he was in a vice grip that was being wound tighter and tighter. After almost seventy-two hours the decline leveled off and the degree of damage could be assessed.

The ICU doctors didn't want to tell Bill how bad off he was so they sent in a psychiatrist who said, "Now look, Chaplain, you've been injured, and you shouldn't expect too much of yourself." Bill replied, "I don't need any of your psycho stuff. Me'n God have got this all worked out. I'm walking out of this hospital, and I'm going to just go on."

That psychiatrist was trying to prepare Bill for something that he wasn't ready to hear.

Bill's dream job was over. He was going to be medically retired from the navy. And thus, Bill's spiritual struggle began. He questioned God about the deal they had. The one where God would and did see him through college and seminary, and where God saw him through the mandatory pastorate he needed in order to be endorsed by his denomination. Everything had lined up for him. Bill wasn't supposed to be called to active duty, but a fine Catholic chaplain took a liking to him, and he suddenly had orders . . . everything lined up so there was no way in Bill's mind that he was not supposed to be a military chaplain. He refused to receive the news that his job was over. He said, "No, guys, I don't care what you say; I'm getting through this!"

The navy sent Bill home to be with Tangela and to start three months of rehabilitation work. The first month did not go well because Bill was unteachable. He wouldn't listen to anything the therapist had to say because he already knew that he and God had the whole deal worked out. His attitude wasn't entirely his fault; another side effect of the stroke was that it heightened the "I can do anything I put my mind to" part of Bill's personality, so it made accepting reality even more difficult.

About the second month Bill began to realize that he wasn't getting any better. He had long-term and short-term memory problems. He had speech problems, and he couldn't find words he was looking for. His deficits were becoming more apparent with each passing day, and Bill began to feel sorry for himself. He was getting depressed and angry and had demanding one-way conversations with God: "Why did you save me? You had a chance to kill me, why didn't you? God, it would have been better if you'd just killed me instead of leaving me like this because I'm not anything like I was." Bill was struggling spiritually and was having a hard time praying. He could barely read Scripture because all he could think was, *God, why? Why did you bring me to this point?*

Bill felt abandoned. He thought he was going to end up being a recluse in his house because he couldn't imagine letting people see his deficits. He thought of himself as "damaged goods." The navy didn't want him anymore, and he wasn't being a very good dad, or a very good husband. He had a short fuse, a bad temper, and he yelled and screamed all the time. Even his dog didn't like him. What was to like? Bill's self-confidence had been stripped away. He had become angry, brooding, and malcontent.

He was no longer independent. Before his stroke, Bill had never depended on anybody in his entire life. Suddenly he had to have somebody drive him places. Like me, Bill needed help with his medication because he would get confused about which pill to take and when. His inability to take care of himself made him feel worthless and useless, and he really didn't want to live. He says he knew his family didn't sign up for it, but they'd gotten a new dad and a new husband—a brain-damaged one. His thoughts spiraled downward, *If the navy doesn't want me, who is going to want me? What kind of skills do I have? I've trained seven years to be a minister, and who's going to want a brain-damaged preacher?*

Bill remembers that it was during his rehabilitation that he realized God had not caused his stroke, but He had allowed it to happen. That's when Bill started trying to see things through God's eyes. As he looked back over his life, Bill could see that he always had to be in control. Even though he said he was called to the ministry, as soon as he thought he knew what God wanted, Bill said, "God, you're either coming with me or you're in the way, but I've got it now, I've got it!"

And he began to tell God how they were going to get it done. Bill believes that in God's great mercy and love He stepped back and said, *Well, you just go right ahead, Bill!*

From anyone else's perspective it probably appeared that Bill was doing a good job. He was being promoted, he was going to get another set of orders, people liked him, and things were great. But the stroke made it impossible for him to be like he used to be, and Bill began to think that maybe, just maybe, that was the point. Maybe God didn't want him to be like he was. The very thing that made him successful—as a chaplain, as a go-getter, as someone who could compete at any level—was also a curse. Bill had always done everything Bill wanted to do by relying on Bill, and leaving God out in the cold.

Between God's grace and his wife's love, Bill did get to the point where he can thank God for his stroke. He knows now that he was such a prideful man, and so dependent on what he could do, that he really wasn't doing anything for God. He was talking about God, but he wasn't serving Him. Bill is so grateful God loved him enough to give him a second chance to serve Him. Now he knows who He is, and he depends on God, not himself. He goes to hospitals and nursing homes and visits stroke victims, paraplegics, and people who are depressed. He can minister to them with confidence because he knows, "If you're still breathing, God is not done with you yet!" God's light can shine through Bill because it is obvious that he still loves life and isn't concerned about his deficits. When Bill tells them, "In Christ, you can do all things through Him who strengthens you," he knows it is true. He also tells them that "There's hope in Christ, and if you'll just let Christ be who He is, which is your healer, your friend, your advocate, and the lover of your soul, if you'll just let Christ be that for you, you'll discover that you still have purpose."

Bill Blain has survived his spiritual struggle. These days, when Bill stands before his congregation (he's a full-time pastor) and he can't find a word he's looking for, the congregation starts yelling out options, and soon enough, Bill is preaching full-speed ahead.

You Can Depend on God

Life viewed through spiritual eyes takes on a whole new meaning. The valleys don't seem as deep, and the mountaintop experiences are awash with gratitude. Both valleys and mountaintops are heavenly gifts from God. With faith, foundational peace persists in the face of chaos, and every tomorrow holds hope. I cannot encourage you enough to know Jesus. He will make your life worth living. If you are having a spiritual struggle or know someone who is, I have a testimonial CD I'd like to send you about my spiritual experience. Contact Laurie Magers at lmagers@ziglar.com to request your free copy.

13

Struggles with Illness and Grief

Medicine has changed tremendously since I was a child. When my father died of a cerebral hemorrhage brought on by a malarial infection, he had been suffering from headaches for a while and even blacked out occasionally, but he did not go to the doctor. You had to be seriously ill before money would be spent on a doctor's visit. Obviously, the concept of "seriously ill" has changed since my father's lifetime. I say that to say this: the medical help we get today prolongs life and has changed the lives of the survivors and those who care for them.

My father was only forty-eight years old when he died, but there was no prolonged, drawn-out period of suffering and illness. The means to keep him alive did not exist at that time. Our family was left to grieve and learn how to go on without him, but we were not called upon to provide hands-on care for him in a debilitated state for several years while we struggled to go on living without his usual contributions to the family.

These days more people than ever survive medical emergencies and end up requiring lots of hands-on, long-term care. Dennis Faulkner did, and his wife, Marilyn, filled the gap for him. You will be touched as you read about Marilyn and Dennis Faulkner's loving relationship and how a massive heart attack changed their lives for eternity.

Laura Johnson (Reichert) knows all too well the incredible strain Alzheimer's disease can put on the individual who has it, as well as on the family's emotional and financial resources. Her plea for change and her family's struggle with Alzheimer's disease will penetrate your heart. Read on to discover the struggles and the blessings of the "bonus years."

Dennis and Marilyn Faulkner

Dennis Faulkner stood out in a crowd, even when he was sitting down! His height of six foot nine wasn't what drew my attention to him. It was all the careful, loving attention he was getting from his smiling and cheerful wife, Marilyn! And, I have to admit, they were sitting with a very happy and enthusiastic bunch of friends who were just a little bit on the loud side. They were having so much fun laughing and talking that it made me and my girls want to go sit on their side of the auditorium.

All of us had gathered in Tennessee in the Gatlinburg Convention Center for our traditional Memorial Day weekend with Bill and Gloria Gaither and their crew to celebrate Family Fest in the Smokies. The year was 2004. Dennis and Marilyn were on their fourth trip to

Family Fest, and the Redhead, Cindy, Julie, and I were on our eighth as a family. We all exchanged smiles several times until we finally went over to find out what the beaming wife and the grinning guy in the big wheelchair were so happy about. I can't recall when I've ever been to a better gratitude meeting in my life!

Dennis and Marilyn were practically tripping over each other's words, telling us how blessed and fortunate they were. Dennis had survived a massive heart attack and an extremely risky quadruple bypass in April 2002. The doctors said they almost lost Dennis a few times during the surgery and had to zap him once before he left the operating room. Later, when Dennis asked the doctor how close it had been, the doctor asked, "How close can it get?"

I never would have guessed at how difficult things really were for Dennis and Marilyn because all they could talk about was how blessed they were. When Marilyn sent us the information we requested so that we could include their story in this book, I was even more amazed at the joy I witnessed at our first meeting. When I read it, I finally understood why Dennis was in a wheelchair when we met. He had lost about 70 percent of his heart's function between the heart attack and the bypass surgery, and he was dealing with congestive heart failure. His heart was so devastated that Dennis was never able to go back to work. He also had damage to his vocal chords, probably due to the breathing tube that was in his throat for five days, and had difficulty speaking and swallowing.

Forty-four days after he left home in an ambulance, Dennis returned. The struggle was really just beginning. Dennis wasn't able to drive for a year. He needed a walker or a wheelchair to get around. Marilyn, who tells me she does not have a servant's heart by nature, had to learn to be a servant in order to take care of Dennis. She said she clung to Philippians 4:13, "I can do all things through Christ who strengthens me" (NKJV), and that God's strength carried her through.

She gave Dennis his showers, changed his wound dressings, and emptied the commode every day when she got home from work. She made pudding so Dennis could more easily swallow his pills and she loaded up the weekly pill boxes. She also gave Dennis shots when he needed them.

Since he couldn't drive or talk, Marilyn went to every doctor's appointment with Dennis and took an active role in managing his care. (The doctors loved Marilyn's medication spreadsheet!) She told me there were plenty of times when it was inconvenient for her to take care of Dennis, but she learned what she had to do and how to do it with joy and thankfulness in her heart. She was glad to do all that she could for the man she loved.

So many health challenges were faced over the next few years . . . Dennis got a staph infection, then the doctors ruled out surgery to repair Dennis's voice because it was just too risky to put him under anesthesia. God, Marilyn pointed out, chose to show His sense of humor and restore Dennis's voice when he got a really bad cold. Then Dennis went into the hospital for a heart-related treatment and developed a very painful problem with his gallbladder. After every effort to handle the problem without risky surgery, it had to be removed. He was evaluated twice (two different insurance companies) and turned down twice for a heart transplant. His diabetes made him a poor risk—they had to save the hearts for the people most likely to survive a transplant. He couldn't sleep, he couldn't qualify for any clinical trials, and eventually fluid had to be drawn off his lungs and then his legs. His heart just couldn't keep up with its job.

But Dennis never quit living, and neither did Marilyn. They got the most out of the time they had after Dennis's health failed. They saw the love of God in the many things that were done for them. Their precious next-door neighbor, Missy, washed clothes for Marilyn so she wouldn't be faced with that job when she finally got home from the hospital each night. When Dennis was housebound, Missy's son Asher carried the mail into "Mr. Dennis" and delivered handmade cards as well. Both Marilyn's and Dennis's places of employment were wonderful during and after the hospital stay. A friend volunteered to come to the house to cut Dennis's hair. Two men from their church took turns driving him to his cardiac rehab appointments so Marilyn wouldn't miss more time from work. Even the Bible study they had attended began to meet at Dennis and Marilyn's house so Dennis could continue to participate.

Marilyn told me that the blessings were many. She and Dennis grew closer as a couple and closer to the Lord. They learned to appreciate each day and each other in a way that wouldn't have been possible had they not gone through so much together. They knew the only reason Dennis was still alive was because the Lord had a purpose for him, and they couldn't wait to find out what it was. When the days seemed the darkest, they learned how wonderful their friends, neighbors, and family truly were. And they discovered they had people praying for them all over the world, many of whom they'd never met.

From the outset Dennis told everyone he wasn't worried at all because he knew that God was in control, no matter what the outcome. He was at peace. Marilyn found Isaiah 41:13 to be the biggest help to her. It says, "I am the LORD, your God, who takes hold of your right hand and says to you, Do not fear; I will help you" (NIV). She said it was such a visual to her—God reaching down to take her hand and help her, just like a father does with a child. And just like a child, she clung to the hand God extended to her.

When we saw Marilyn and Dennis again at Family Fest in 2005, they were still hanging out with that huge bunch of fun people from their church and having a good time. But when we saw Marilyn at Family Fest in 2006, our hearts fell. Dennis wasn't with her, and we knew. "Oh, Marilyn, when did you lose him? We're so sorry." Nothing could have prepared us for her answer, "Dennis died last Friday, May 19."

It had only been one full week, and Marilyn said she knew it would probably seem strange to some but everyone thought that she should come. We understood; the Redhead and I had gone to Family Fest less than two weeks after our daughter Suzan died. Going there is like being with your huge family in Christ, and the music ministers to your aching soul. Marilyn told us they had the memorial service on May 23, and she couldn't imagine staying home and being miserable when her best friends and her support group were all going to be at Family Fest. Her mother and her sister, in an effort to support Marilyn, had made the trip to Gatlinburg as well. We knew Marilyn was crying and singing, praising God and missing Dennis. She was in exactly the right place.

God had been with Marilyn every step of the way through Dennis's heart attack, so she knew that she could count on Him to help her after Dennis died. He had been her strength before. . . . He would not abandon her as she grieved. She said that she found church services to be the most difficult for her. She loved singing songs and praising God, but that was the hardest thing in the world to do. She'd start wondering what heaven must be like for Dennis, what he'd be doing, and then she'd have to make herself stop thinking.

She missed him so much. She had spent hour upon hour caring for him over the past four years. Her role as his caregiver eventually defined who she was, and suddenly he was gone. Marilyn no longer felt needed. She couldn't call him on her way home from work, and silence met her at the door when she arrived, so she found herself avoiding going home. Instead, she worked late or went to the gym or shopping. And she felt guilty for wanting to be in heaven more so she could see Dennis than see Jesus. Adjusting to her new lifestyle was going to take time.

Marilyn attended a grief-recovery program called GriefShare (I am honored to be a small part of GriefShare and highly recommend you visit www.griefshare.org to learn more about this ministry) and learned much about how to cope with her grief, but her mother proved to be her best resource. Her mother had lost a son in a helicopter crash in 1986 and her husband in a car accident in 1988. A verse given to her daughter-in-law when her son died has become a comfort to Marilyn: "Since the Lord is directing our steps, why try to understand everything that happens along the way?" (Proverbs 20:24 TLB). Marilyn told me that she may never understand why everything happened the way it did, but she doesn't have to keep searching for answers when she has the Lord to direct her steps. She says she doesn't think in terms of "woulda', coulda', shoulda'," because she knows God is in control.

Marilyn is swift to correct people when they remark on how strong she is and how well she is dealing with her loss. She tells them it is not her strength, but her dependence on God that gets her through the days, weeks, and months. Marilyn says she can't comprehend how people who don't have a personal relationship with Jesus Christ deal with death and grieving. She is confident of where Dennis is because of his decision to accept Christ as his Savior at the age of fifty. She says, "As a Christian, I have *a hope* that I will see Dennis in heaven. Not that I *hope* I will see him (like I hope it won't rain tomorrow), but that I *have a hope* that is founded in God's truth, which is why I have confidence." That *hope* is her comfort in the midst of her grief.

A sermon titled "How Will It All End?" was preached on June 25, 1995, the day Dennis Faulkner asked Jesus to be his Lord and Savior. The major points of that very sermon were preached again at one of his two memorial services. Marilyn told me it is difficult to explain to people how you can grieve and be full of joy at the same time. She doesn't think it is humanly possible, yet that is exactly how she felt at both of Dennis's memorial services. She is grateful for the "four bonus years" she and Dennis shared, and she knows he is with our Lord and Savior, whole and healthy, and she will see him again some-day. Dennis Faulkner's life honored his Lord. I saw how he adored and honored his wife; and I think it is safe to say that Dennis Faulkner's life ended well, very well, indeed!

Laura Johnson (Reichert)

Laura Johnson has had family die of heart attacks. She has had more people than she can count on both sides of her family die from cancer. In fact, one year cancer claimed the lives of her favorite aunt, her favorite uncle, and that same uncle's daughter, all within a few months. As horrible and sad as all of that was, she tells me that *"nothing"* is as painful or horrible as watching someone you love go through the dying process with the disease of Alzheimer's.

Laura's family started noticing some changes in her mom around the beginning of 2004. Her mother had always been incredibly smart when it came to remembering names and dates. It definitely was a gift with her. But that year she started to hesitate or occasionally not come up with anything at all. She would clench her fists in frustration, but her family knew that happened to everyone, so at first they didn't think too much about it.

But as the year went on, Laura's mother, who was sixty-nine at this time, seemed to be getting more and more forgetful of dates. And they did start to notice. Each one of the five kids recognized something was changing, but for most of that year they didn't really say very much to one another beyond a comment here or there about how unusual it was for their mother to forget dates.

Then came Thanksgiving 2004. Seldom were all five of the kids together, but that year after her parents had gone home, the siblings sat in their sister's living room, waiting for one of them to be brave enough to bring it up. Finally, the unspeakable was spoken: their mom was getting Alzheimer's.

Their maternal grandmother had gotten Alzheimer's years earlier, and Laura well remembered the first time her mother came back from the nursing home brokenhearted and told them what had happened. When she had entered her mother's room, she announced, "Mama, it's Nina here." Her mother looked up and said, "I used to have a daughter named Nina." Laura said it was sad for her and her siblings to see their mother suffer because of the condition of their grandmother, but at that time it didn't strike them how awful it really was.

The following year Laura and her siblings finally talked to their dad to see if he knew what was going on. He said he knew and that it really had been going on for a few years longer than they knew about but that their mom had been very good at hiding it.

As that year continued on, Laura's mother really began to descend into the disease, and her father became somewhat of a prisoner in his own home. With tears in his eyes, Laura's usually stoic father told about the first really scary incident. Her mother had poured herself a glass of water to take her daily medications. She had the bottle of pills in one hand and the water in the other and she couldn't remember what she was supposed to do with either. From that day forward he had to be present when his wife took her medicine to make sure she did it correctly.

Laura said more and more incidents occurred. Her mom would pick up her toothbrush and not know what to do with it. She would put toothpaste on her comb because she knew she had to use both items but couldn't remember how they worked or what they did. She would get so frustrated that she clenched her fists and at times even banged them on the table.

Finally, about the middle of 2005, Laura's mother knew exactly what was happening to her and decided to let others know. She called her sisters and her best friend and told them she had Alzheimer's. Laura said it was extremely hard for her and so hard on them, too, because they had no idea her mind was failing her. They all lived out of town, so they didn't see it when they would visit because her mom could hide the symptoms for those short periods of time.

Then Laura's mom got cancer too. The disease ravaged her body, making her lose much weight and all of her energy. And the Alzheimer's became worse because of it. Sometimes she knew she had cancer and it was in her breasts, and she knew she did not want them removed. So she fought her cancer with radiation and chemotherapy. Other times, Laura's mother didn't understand why they kept hurting her.

Laura said the hard part got worse each week. Her mother could no longer read, and she couldn't stand to have the television on because she couldn't follow the story line any longer. And she could not stand for Laura's father to be gone; she would get panicky and angry if he left. If he talked to anyone on the phone too long, she would just stare at him, imploring him to get off the phone. If he fell asleep, which he tended to do more and more because the strain was wearing him out so badly, she would stand by his chair and stare down at him or shake him awake (she was just so scared when he was not there "with" her because he was sleeping).

Laura's dad had loved to go to church every Sunday. Even when the family was traveling on vacation, he would find a church and go. But he stopped when his wife didn't want to anymore because she couldn't follow the sermon. The only person Laura's mom would leave the house with, and then only on a few occasions, was Laura's sister, Kathy. So Laura's father got very few breaks from his 24/7 vigil of caregiving.

On the occasions that they *could* get Laura's mom out of the house, it was amazing that, considering everything she forgot, she did not forget her pride. Though she weighed a little over ninety pounds and could hardly walk, she refused every wheelchair offer she ever got, and there were plenty of them! What is the one struggling with the struggler to do? Respect the wishes of the struggler if at all possible.

By Thanksgiving of 2005 Laura's mother was getting so weak and so tired that her mind would not let her concentrate much at all. She would just kind of fade out. She might be in the room with ten others, but it was obvious she wasn't seeing anything. Then she would come back for a while. Her family sadly took in the bitter truth—they were losing her one day at a time.

Then the cancer came back. Laura's parents had already signed a living will stating that neither of them wanted to be kept alive on machines, and fortunately her mother was present enough mentally to say that she did not want to go through chemo and radiation again. They all knew they didn't want to prolong her descent into Alzheimer's and accepted her choice to do nothing to prolong her life.

In April of 2006, Laura's mom suffered a fall and broke her hip. Unfortunately, her mother's main doctor was out of town and her father didn't know what else to do, so he called 911. The hospital didn't know about the previous decisions regarding her mother's care, and they performed hip-replacement surgery. For a few days after the surgery she still seemed to know who people were. But then they moved her to a nursing home, and she didn't understand why she was in so much pain. It was more than she could take, and her mind was totally gone. She no longer knew her own family, and her pain caused her to cry out for her mama. She was scared and didn't understand anything that was happening to her.

For ten days her loved ones struggled as they watched her suffer. She forgot how to eat. She didn't know how to chew or swallow. Because of the living will (a document her family remained grateful for because it kept her agony from being prolonged), they could not feed her through tubes. The first several days she just cried out in pain. Then in the last few days she mostly just slept. She was going further and further away until finally she forgot how to breathe. The nurse came in and said her heart was still beating but then her heart forgot how to beat. She was gone.

There is so much more to this story, but not all of it will be told. The heartbreak and sadness Laura and her family, and others who have walked through the darkness that is Alzheimer's, have suffered is incalculable. For Laura's family, and others I'm sure, there were times of anger, frustration, uncertainty, and so much more that her mother went through. Laura wants people to know that they are not alone when they deal with Alzheimer's. She wants to see the day when we put as much money, time, and energy into Alzheimer's research as we put into cancer research.

Laura wants the world to know that losing a person while he or she is still alive is the hardest thing in the world. She doesn't think anyone who hasn't experienced it can understand the emptiness and fear that go along with Alzheimer's. She also referenced more times than I could put in her story how exhausted her father was from being the primary caregiver of her mother. There has to be a better way to relieve some of the burden for those who attempt to care for their loved ones at home.

Grieving is a process that begins well before the death of an individual who is dying from Alzheimer's disease. I can imagine that many families who lose their loved one to Alzheimer's feel relieved for the one they lost and might even struggle emotionally for feeling that way: few support groups are as needed as Alzheimer's support groups. If your family is dealing with this tragic and incurable disease, I strongly encourage you to get help. Our family has a taste of what it is to have a family member with short-term memory loss, and we know we are experiencing just a fraction of what Alzheimer's and other forms of dementia ultimately lead to.

I am grateful Laura shared her walk and her family's walk through their struggle with her mother's disease. I hope that everyone who has read this story will have more compassion for those suffering from Alzheimer's and will have a much better understanding of the toll this disease can take on caregivers. Hopefully, it will serve as an encouragement to reach out and help families in need.

14

Life on Life's Terms

There is a great deal of practical information on living life on life's terms at the beginning of this book, especially in chapter 3, "To Embrace Is to Accept," and I encourage you to go back and review it for details on how you can do that for yourself. Here you will find true life application of living life on life's terms in the stories of individuals who I think are doing an incredible job of living life right where they are to the very fullest.

Jodie Butler's story is multifaceted and allows us to see three distinctly different examples of life on life's terms. Bill McArthur's journey from suicidal depression to a life filled with God-given purpose shows how life's terms, as harsh as they were, broke him out of an unhealthy existence. Through the story of Laurel Marshall we will learn how our struggles and differences make us unique and even cause us to excel!

Jodie Butler

Jim Butler

According to Jodie Butler, God allowed him to make a choice. He could "either embrace the struggle or let the problem become all-consuming." He learned at an early age that obstacles could be overcome. When he was ten years old his father, Jim Butler, had a severe brain injury that resulted in a coma. When his dad finally did come home, he was only a fraction of the father little Jodie had known. He was entirely paralyzed on the left side of his body and had absolutely zero balance. His short-term memory was gone; he did not know who he was, much less who Jodie was. The doctors had warned the family that Mr. Butler would be in a vegetative state—and judging from what Jodie saw, they were probably right.

Jodie would watch his father for hours, lying there in the bed trying to make his lifeless muscles move. He would take his left hand in his right and lift it up and drop it. Lift and drop. Lift and drop. A thousand times a day it seemed. Lift and drop. Then he would massage the left side of his face trying to feel something . . . anything. Every day little Jodie prayed the Lord would let his dad see improvement.

After months of persistent effort Jim Butler's finger twitched. Then his hand jumped. Jim improved gradually until he was able to walk again. Jodie Butler's dad knew that life on life's terms didn't mean that he had to give up just because a doctor said it was hopeless. He knew that at that moment he had to do what he could to make a difference in his circumstances. And his son was watching him.

Many years later, when he was the best man at Jodie's wedding, he drove his family to the church, prayed with Jodie before the ceremony, and walked to the front of the church without a limp. Then, when he was in his seventies, he played in a softball game so Jodie's team wouldn't have to forfeit. Jodie had a really nice hit that night . . . his dad had two. And he hasn't let Jodie forget it, either! Not bad for a "vegetable."

In July of 2007, the doctors had more bad news. They told Jodie's family that his father probably would not live through the night. His dad, once again, respectfully disagreed. Recently, Jodie was honored to walk the hallowed ground of the National World War II Memorial in Washington, DC, with his father and 101 other World War II heroes who saved the free world. Jim Butler has been an inspiration to many people. He faced his trials with strength, dignity, and faith, all the while preparing his watching son for what was to come his way.

Jodie's Trial

Shortly after Jodie married, he began to have memory problems of his own. As it grew worse, large blocks of time couldn't be accounted for. He might have been at work or school and had acted in a completely appropriate manner, but he had zero recollection of the events. Eventually, the stretches of unaccounted-for time became longer in duration and occurred with much greater frequency.

After several frustrating years Jodie's neurologist delivered the news: Jodie had epilepsy. Everyone was relieved to finally have some answers, but having a diagnosis did not immediately provide him with relief. His seizures went from undetectable petite mal to grand mal (full-blown convulsions). At one point, Jodie was having over thirty seizures a day. He didn't work or drive for five years. The emergency room at the local hospital had his wife's work number on the wall in every room. It included a note telling the attending physician not to call her before 3:00 p.m. That way she wouldn't have to miss any more work while he slept off the Valium that was regularly administered to stop his convulsions.

Jodie has been free of convulsions for more than seven years now, but his illness came with great cost. It cost him and his wife financially, it cost him a business, and it cost him the friendship of some people who didn't know how to handle the situation. But through it all God was gracious. Not often did He allow Jodie and his wife to be down at the same time. When one of them was feeling low, the other had strength. Jodie is grateful to God for showing them this kindness.

Jodie credits his recovery to the way God worked through his bride of twenty years. Kristie became the breadwinner, caregiver, all the while remaining a loving wife. She also was an encourager to others experiencing similar situations. Jodie said, "Kristie comes packaged with a servant's heart and the strength of steel. This is wrapped in a layer of elegant, Southern grace. I am blessed."

Jodie never questioned God "why?" but he did at times ask "how long?" He already knew that God had a plan, and he found hope in Matthew 7:9–11, "Which one of you, if his son asks him for bread, will give him a stone? Or if he asks for a fish, will give him a serpent? If you then, who are evil, know how to give good gifts to your children, how much more will your Father who is in heaven give good things to those who ask him!" (ESV). Jodie considers it his job to remember, even if he can't see it at the time, that his illness is a loaf of bread. God doesn't give His children stones.

This has become even more evident in the Butler home the last few years. On December 1, 2005, Jodie lost his brother-in-law, Marine Staff Sergeant Daniel Clay, in Fallujah, Iraq. He told me some thought with certainty Dan would return safely from his second tour. Thirteen months earlier Dan's sister Jennifer had died just seven weeks after the birth of her fourth child. "Surely God wouldn't take Dan after He brought Jennifer 'safely home,'" was the way Jennifer's dad put it. Jodie allowed that God's plan isn't always our plan.

During the 2006 State of the Union address, President Bush quoted from the letter Dan left for his family, in the event of his death. The following Memorial Day, the late Dr. D. James Kennedy aired a special on the family and how the Lord has walked everyone through their losses. This was broadcast worldwide.

The months and now years that have passed have shown Jodie's family how the deaths of two of the people they most loved is bread and not a stone. They will never know how many people have come to Christ as a result. But Jodie can tell you this—some of them that he knows well have come to know Christ *only* because of this. It sometimes takes a life-changing blow to wake us up.

Jodie said, "While Dan was lost on the physical battlefield, his death has been used in a much larger battle—the spiritual battle going on around us every day. Our military is fighting for our protection and freedom, but there is a fight more important than the one for our lives, and that's the fight for our eternity."

Jodie assures me that Jennifer and Dan would have raised their hands and volunteered to go (like Dan did in the Marines) had they known the impact their deaths would ultimately have on God's kingdom. There will be additional loved ones in heaven because of the plan God designed for Jodie's family. Let there be no mistake—it was designed in advance for a cause. As Jodie's mother-in-law said shortly after hearing of Dan's death, "Heaven is looking better all the time."

As Jodie says, "This, friends, is bread!"

I say Jodie has been through a lot of trials and has learned that life on life's terms is livable—when you serve the One from whom life flows.

Bill McArthur

Bill McArthur's life was ebbing instead of flowing. Where he had once found complete and utter joy, he now felt instead physically ill, as wave after wave of helplessness, confusion, and hopelessness swept over him. What he had thought to be true was not, and his body lurched at the magnitude of his discovery. His whole life . . . what had it stood for, been about? How could he, of all people, have been so blindsided? Many were the questions that led him back and forth across the edges of sanity, questions that drove him deeper and deeper into self-examination and doubt. Bill McArthur, a man who had lived to help others avoid suicide was now facing these same frightening questions.

It had all started innocently enough. Bill wanted to be the best he could be. He looked up to his mentors, in awe of their skills and knowledge. The men and women he sought to emulate were the best. They had integrity and compassion. They were highly regarded teachers and supervisors who had exacting standards of ethics and professional care.

Bill read voraciously and was engrossed and captivated by his work. All things work were joy to him. For years he drove each day toward his office, enthused and excited with an expectancy of what the day would bring. He equated the love of his job with what King Solomon wrote in Ecclesiastes 3:13, "Every man should eat and drink, and enjoy the good of all his labour, it is the gift of God" (KJV). Bill lived his toil with pleasure, all day, every day, year in and year out—he loved his work!

He should have seen them, the subtle changes, the warning signs, but it all happened so gradually. Bill's teachers, his mentors and old bosses, retired and gone, replaced by a different sort of person. High standards and integrity, which he and a few others held themselves to,

appeared to be replaced with duplicity; fear, not joy, was the domi-
nating force in his workplace. But Bill only became aware that something was wrong when a colleague stopped him in the hall and asked,
"You do know you are being bullied, don't you?" Shocked and embar-
rassed, Bill mumbled, "Yes, I know," and retreated into his office to
determine why he had ignored the signs. He felt abused, like a victim
of domestic violence. He had encountered maliciousness in what
should have been a safe place.

His body soon began to betray the turmoil that lay within. The
telltale signs of stress manifested in psoriasis on his arms, body, and
scalp. Bill had chronic, persistent diarrhea and felt tired and overly
anxious. He worked harder and harder, double-checking all that he
had done during the day. As he struggled with the turn his life had
taken, he dealt with profound feelings of humiliation and abject
loneliness. He knew he needed help—highly skilled, professional
counseling—but where could he go? He, himself, was a qualified
therapist in several fields for over twenty-five years, and the person
he would normally have sought help and support from to confront
the bully was in fact the person who was abusing him . . . and others.

Bill did get some help, forty sessions' worth. He even went to a
few professional conferences but was too sick to learn or participate
in the conference sessions. His family grieved for the son, the brother,
the husband, and the father they had known. He struggled to live
each day and felt unsure of who he was and if he could be of any use
to anyone anymore. He needed something profoundly different, and
he became willing to step out of his comfort zone to get it. Bill signed
up for four days of motivational training.

The weekend was very good, but there was nothing new being
taught at the seminar. Bill himself had used much of the information
in working with his own clients, but he did hear one thing different,
my name. He was not impressed! Bill actually thought Zig Ziglar was

probably another eastern mystic, but he could not forget my name. He eventually bought a copy of *See You at the Top* (as cheaply as he could) and wasn't impressed with the title of my book either.

He was, however, relieved when the book arrived to find my picture on the back and to discover that I am a conventional, all-American, clean-cut, executive type . . . no beads! Bill had always put his stock in books from his chosen fields, counseling, psychology, and psychotherapy. He considered self-help books to be secondary to the academic and scholarly works he preferred. But his life was in chaos and nothing made sense, so Bill decided he didn't have anything to lose.

At the risk of sounding like I'm tooting my own horn, I'm going to share with you what Bill said he learned. You just have to remember that everything I teach is based on biblical principles and that the truth, even in parable form, has power that people's best intellectual ideas will never have. Bill said that my book "told it how it is" and "affirmed" who he, in his "brokenness," was. He felt that I connected with him and "became the friend he'd never met." He said that I "spoke with authority," and that "I disciplined his character with love." Bill came to know the power of genuine and unconditional love and acceptance.

Bill was encouraged. His thinking and his behavior were challenged, and many of his preconceptions began to shift. With that shift came a new openness to listen to what Scripture said, along with my book and his Daily Notes, all three of which seemed to connect. Suddenly, Bill McArthur felt affirmed and is now driven with a purpose. His difficulties didn't magically disappear, but his "loser's limp" did! He began to take ownership of his own shortcomings, like making his work his idol and having an elevated opinion of himself in his "specialized services," and to recognize that it was through his weakness and brokenness that he was becoming stronger, that strength is God-given and given for a purpose.

Bill's life had once been filled with that which was inadequate and pretentious, and it resulted in life terms that were miserable. But he is grateful for his brokenness; without it he would never have discovered that life "underpinned with truth, rooted in faith, and crowned with compassionate love, is biblical and principled." Bill has chosen faith, integrity, and compassion as his passport to better living. He can't control what others do, but he can make the next right choice for himself.

Laurel Marshall

"Take her home and enjoy her . . . she will not live past the age of two." This was the paralyzing pronouncement from the doctors to Laurel Marshall's devastated parents. Even the best doctors were perplexed by what ailed the tiny blond toddler, and getting a semiconfirmed diagnosis of muscular dystrophy took a long time. Laurel's parents never let on how horrified they were, and they decided immediately that they would hold her to a high standard and keep her accountable for her actions. Laurel says, "Their expectations were wrapped up in constant love and support and tied up with a strong faith in God."

One day at a time it became obvious that the doctors were wrong in their dire prediction. Laurel flew past the ages of two, ten, twenty, thirty . . . she probably would like for me to stop there, and I will, but she is living life fully on life's terms, not the doctors'. Laurel believed it when her parents taught her there wasn't anything she could not do. In fact, Laurel has dedicated her life to teaching and gives credit to her parents' natural ability to teach and to her disability. There was no persuasion, just a natural progression toward the career she is passionate about.

All of her life Laurel has been told by both friends and strangers that she is an inspiration to them. It was hard for her to understand and even embarrassing in her younger years. Her parents had always made her feel normal, so Laurel thought she was just like anyone else. In reality, she was not. Muscular dystrophy made walking difficult. In the seventh grade, she had to get crutches and braces for her legs in order to walk. In the eighth grade, she fell and broke her hip. That incident put her in a wheelchair for good. Her muscle weakness also affected her hands, leaving them with an inability to grasp. But, Laurel, as a child, was determined not to stand out, and she found a way to do what everyone else was doing, even if she had to do it in an unconventional way. There were no other options. She just did what she had to do. And she still does.

During her years at Texas A&M University, Laurel became more and more convinced that her major (and, thus, her profession) had to be one that she could feel passionate about, one that would inspire others. She wanted to pass on the lessons that her parents taught her: having high expectations, a positive attitude, high self-esteem, along with accountability for one's actions. She wanted to pass on life skills such as perseverance, empathy, compassion, and patience. In return she wanted to receive the joy she felt from sharing the values that defined her life. After several false starts, Laurel knew she had found her passion the day she enrolled as an elementary-education teacher. She followed her dream to completion and has even been honored as the 2005–06 Richardson Independent School District Teacher of the Year.

Laurel believes that every child can be successful in school and that teachers play a pivotal role in that success. She carefully creates an atmosphere in her fourth-grade classroom that makes her students feel they are in a warm, safe, happy environment. Her room has bright, cheery walls and is filled with stuffed animals from her childhood. She provides consistent structure and routines, knowing that children need to know what to expect in order to feel secure. Flexibility is a must, as is being fair and listening to her students, qualities that are important to any child. Laurel tells me she tries to follow the Golden Rule by treating her students as she wants to be treated. She puts herself in their shoes, lending empathy, understanding, and, if they stumble, a soft place to fall. Her high expectations hold each child accountable to be his or her personal best.

Those beliefs and qualities make Laurel an outstanding teacher, but they are not what sets her apart. What makes her distinct is that she is able to integrate into her curriculum daily life lessons that cannot be found in any lesson plan. Due to her disability, the kids take actively responsible roles in the classroom. They act as her hands and feet, without judgment. From picking up a dropped chalk holder, setting up the overhead projector, or racing to grab her key so they can be the first person to lock her purse away in her closet, they are happy to help. Laurel says children have a natural spirit of giving, and she never takes their acts of kindness for granted. She makes it a point to let them know how much she appreciates them.

Laurel Marshall also makes it a point to give her time and efforts to organizations that made a difference in her life. After graduation Laurel was honored to return to her alma mater as a Texas A&M Fish Camp speaker (Fish Camp is new-student orientation), sharing her experiences and helping to pass on the feeling of acceptance she had received so many years before. In 1990 she was one of Texas A&M's Multicultural Convention panel speakers and a part of Texas A&M's Handicapped Accessibility committee. Through both roles Laurel was able to enhance disability awareness on campus.

Normally, people think of the handicapped as being the recipients of others' volunteer efforts. However, when Laurel Marshall is involved, the tables are turned. Through the years, the Muscular Dystrophy Association (MDA) supported Laurel by providing her with crutches, wheelchairs, and medical equipment. She was thrilled and honored to be their Women's Leadership Luncheon keynote speaker in 1999. In 2000, she wholeheartedly accepted MDA's invitation to be the honorary chairperson for their annual "Cruisin' to a Cure" benefit. Then she became a devoted committee member for that event for the next four years, helping to raise tens of thousands of dollars for MDA.

One of her favorite volunteer jobs was attending MDA summer camp as a motivational speaker from 2000 through 2002. In that role, she spoke to disabled teenagers about life, college, and their favorite topic—dating! She tried to convey to them simple but important messages: believe in yourself, set goals, and keep a positive attitude to achieve them. One year she also taught wheelchair dancing. By the end of the session, the campers had new "boogie-woogie" attitudes and personal dance techniques designed just for them. The night of the big dance a lot of campers were being asked to dance, and with their new confidence and skills they accepted the invitations. What a tremendous night! The expressions of joy on the faces of the campers convinced Laurel they would treasure memories of that dance forever.

In the summer of 1997, Canine Companions for Independence (CCI) invited Laurel to attend team training in Oceanside, California, where she received her first service dog, Temecula. After returning to Dallas, she helped establish and build CCI's Dallas steering committee, providing support to puppy raisers and future graduates. She was also a volunteer in the Paws to Go dog ministry from 2001 through 2003. There she assisted with dog testing, using the significant training she had received as a service-dog owner to determine if the dogs had the proper obedience skills and temperament to visit the elderly, for whom she has a special heart, in nursing homes.

It is through Laurel's association with CCI that my daughter Cindy, a therapy-dog enthusiast and avid volunteer, met Laurel. An instantaneous friendship developed and, fortunately, Cindy shared her great new friend with the rest of our family. Laurel may have to speak softly because of the physical limitations of her muscular dystrophy, but our house gets really loud when Laurel is there playing dominos with us! Her sense of humor is over the top, and she particularly loves to harass my son-in-law Jim, who in turns dishes it right back. Their mock rivalry at the dominos table is legendary in our family! Any place Laurel is, is a happier, brighter place because she is there, my house included!

You've been reading Laurel's story for a while now. It has to be apparent to you that Laurel fully lives life on life's terms. (How long is your list of accomplishments? How many volunteer efforts have you made?) She was born with a disability, and with the help of her parents she put her efforts into refining her abilities. Laurel will tell you that her differences are what make her unique—and they have caused her to excel. Most important, they have given her her passion. Laurel went into teaching "to become rich—rich with knowledge, rich with smiles and hugs, rich with the ability to inspire others, and rich with the hope of making a difference in the world." She is richer than most, by far, and she has given each child that has passed through her classroom an inheritance that can be passed from one generation to the next. Let me explain.

Laurel's students have to deal with her daily as a disabled person. Those circumstances build acceptance through personal connection and make it possible for them to see beyond the wheelchair, to see her worth as a person. By the time Laurel's students graduate from her class, they know that everyone, including themselves, has worth, dignity, and value. They know that differences are to be celebrated, not feared. Laurel prays that they take the life-changing lessons she teaches them to heart and that they will live them deeply throughout their lives.

I pray that you'll embrace your struggle with the grace and dignity Laurel displays in her life. Life on life's terms is rewarding, and as I said earlier, well worth living!

15

The Future Is in God's Hands

We're nearing the end of this book, but none of us has seen the end of our struggles. My friend and mentor, Fred Smith, died on August 17, 2007. He was ninety-one years wonderful and had struggles clear down to the finish line. I learned more about how to embrace the struggle from watching him live the last three years of his life than I learned during the first twenty years of our friendship. And that was substantial, as you well know if you've read any of my previous books. Fred Smith had a huge influence on my life.

Never once in all the time I knew him did Fred Smith do anything other than embrace his struggles. I saw how he treasured and cared for Mary Alice, his beloved wife of sixty-seven years, as Parkinson's disease slowly took them toward their last good-bye in 2004. I watched him adjust to life without her, wondering how I would ever survive such an incomprehensible loss. In awe of his deep faith and profound contentedness, I pledged anew to be more like him.

Where Fred was concerned, I was always taking notes. He had been called by God to mentor others, and he did all he could for those God put in his path. Anyone under his tutelage emerged better fit to serve God and to serve people. Fred inspired others to higher levels of integrity and helped them see how God would use them if they'd let Him. Many a ministry was born as Fred's wise questions led to head-slapping V8 moments of truth. His discernment was legendary. As was his longevity.

Doctors told Fred he had eighteen months to live eight years before he died. He enjoyed funnies like that. I can't remember the number of times his daughter Brenda Smith called to say it looked like the end was near. We'd all rally round, gather at his bedside, and next thing we knew, Fred had an audience and he'd fight his way back for more years of doing what God had for him to do.

Fred fulfilled his purpose no matter what the circumstances were. He mentored in his hospital room, over the phone, even at dialysis. He'd ask people to join him at "Dialysis University" for his three-to-four-times-a-week appointments, and he'd mentor them while the machines did their job of keeping him alive for a few more days. When he was too ill to leave the house, he'd invite anyone who wanted to come to join him on Saturday mornings for what became known as "Fred in the Bed." He'd be propped up in his bed so he could hold court. The visitors would ask questions, and Fred would answer them. Many days there was standing room only. His daughter Brenda helped him start a website named BreakfastWithFred.com so Fred could mentor people all over the world, and that led to his last book—you guessed it, *Breakfast with Fred.*

Fred once told me how interesting it was adjusting to each new insult he suffered as his body betrayed him. But in true Fred fashion he went on to laughingly say, "I'm not disabled—I'm delightfully dependent." Little by little Fred lost all of his independence until he depended completely on others for every need. In his "memorial message" (yes, Fred even held court, via DVD, at his own remembrance service), he said, "Dear friends, it just wouldn't be natural to have this good assembly of people and me not say a few words." And he was absolutely right! Fred said that a friend told him the difference between a problem and a fact of life: "A problem is something you can do something about. If you can't do anything about it, it's a fact of life, and so we accept facts; we solve problems." Fred accepted the fact that his body failed him. His family and friends helped Fred find ways to solve the problems his failing body presented. There were, however, three things that never failed him: his mind, his family, and God.

God was One of the ones Fred had to learn to be totally dependent on, and he talked about that in his memorial message as well. Fred said, "God doesn't give you strength to overcome. He gives you strength as you overcome." Fred said all he had to do was start; and as he would start doing the things he should do, God would give him the energy to finish what he'd started. Just as I have experienced it, Fred said he often would feel better at the end of his task than he did at the beginning. God was faithful in sending the energy Fred needed as he overcame.

In his memorial message Fred went on to say, "I've had my share of valleys. I've had my share of years of disability. But the thing that I appreciate is that thought, 'never lose the good of a bad experience.' In every bad experience there's something good."

The Good in My Bad Experience

I'm going to take Fred's parting advice and find all the good in my bad experience. It isn't hard, really. It ranges from more time with my family to a whole new outlook for our company. It has brought me to a place where individuals who couldn't relate to me in the past can relate to me now. I have been reminded of how faithful God is, and I've been greatly blessed by the outpouring of love and concern by those who have read my books or listened to me speak.

I've watched with parental pride as my children have stepped up and taken even more active roles in our company, and I rest easy knowing that they have my best interest and the best interest of the company at heart. I've seen our employees step up to the plate as well and embrace the struggle that goes with my speaking less often than I used to. Many have made personal sacrifices because of my circumstances, and I love and appreciate each of them.

I have always been infatuated with that beautiful redheaded wife of mine, but I stand amazed as I consider what she has taken on as a result of my accident. As always, she has embraced our situation with grace. Her quiet strength is more powerful than anyone suspected, especially me. I had enjoyed thinking I was taking care of her all these years. I do love the Redhead! She is my rock, and she is my joy. This accident has resulted in our time together multiplying exponentially. I can never get too much time with my Redhead.

I have always had a healthy respect for the Redhead's judgment. Her ability to size up a situation and people has given me an unfair advantage our entire married life. Her direction is something I've trusted always, which is so important right now. If I did not have faith in her ability, I would not be totally comfortable with my memory loss. I trust her completely to handle anything and everything I need her to handle. My memories are safe in her hands. I am safe in her company. My gratitude for her has grown steadily throughout all the years we've been together. That is another thing that has not changed.

I spoke earlier in the book about being prepared in advance to embrace your struggles as they come. When you have your spiritual life in focus, your family life will thrive; and when your family life is good, your mind is freed up to apply yourself to the work God has called you to. When you live life in that order, the struggles, when they come, don't undo your world. There will be no meltdowns when you know who you are and Whose you are.

I know who I am and Whose I am. I do live with an attitude of excited anticipation. I can't wait to see what God has for me next. I lean on His promise, "I'll never leave you nor forsake you," and His command, "Let not your heart be troubled." I know that I have been called according to His purposes, and I trust Him in *all* things. Romans 5:3–5—"More than that, we rejoice in our sufferings, knowing that suffering produces endurance, and endurance produces character, and character produces hope, and hope does not put us to shame, because God's love has been poured into our hearts through the Holy Spirit who has been given to us" (ESV)—lets me know that God has even more for me to do, that I am being prepared for what is yet to come, and that grows me toward even more hope for the future.

Embrace the struggle. Accept the facts of your life. Then solve the problems you can solve, asking God all the while to show you what He is growing you toward. Look forward to the harvest, and remember, where there is struggle, there is life!

Acknowledgments

Zig Ziglar

As I have often said, you don't get anywhere in life by yourself. Others are always involved, and the occasion of the completion of this work, *Embrace the Struggle*, is no exception to that rule. Many have helped this book come to fruition—and I apologize in advance in the event I've overlooked anyone. In light of that subject, my short-term memory loss, I pray you will forgive me my shortcomings and accept any oversight as a side effect of the struggle I embrace daily.

I have on many occasions voiced my love and affection, my respect and admiration, for the only woman I have ever loved, my wife of sixty-two years, Jean Abernathy Ziglar, the Redhead. Now more than ever I depend on her. I cannot tell you how much it means to me to have the love of someone I trust so completely. Our lives have changed significantly since my fall down the stairs, and I am grateful beyond words to have the support and encouragement, and the care and devotion, that times like these require. I deeply appreciate all she does for me.

I want to recognize my coauthor, my youngest daughter and the editor of my books these past sixteen years, Julie Ziglar Norman. We've worked together so closely that Julie knows my material almost as well as I do. When I needed someone to interview me onstage, Julie stepped up to the challenge, and we've enjoyed sharing the platform ever since. Overseeing this book and its writing from beginning to end was a natural progression for Julie, and I'm grateful she knows my heart and my intent and that she can recognize a "Zig" story from a mile off.

No book of mine gets out the door without the approval of my treasured executive assistant of more than thirty years, Laurie Magers. Laurie's expertise has made my book writing a joyful, stress-free experience. Invariably she catches what Julie and I miss, and I appreciate her making me look so good even while she juggles my schedule and handles the countless other tasks that go along with my hectic work life. I also appreciate how Laurie helps Julie work with me on our books.

My son Tom Ziglar, CEO of Ziglar, Inc., has taken in stride the changes my fall created for our company. I could not be prouder of how he responded to the special challenges we all faced. Because of his ability to think and achieve change in the midst of our trials, our company is getting stronger by the day. We are exploring new territory and we are superexcited about where we are headed. I've come to love the technology that allows me to reach thousands of people without ever leaving home, and I hope you'll join me sometime on the webinars and webcasts Tom arranges for me.

Other family members deserve mention, as well. My daughter Cindy Ziglar Oates has been working in our customer service and bookkeeping departments for almost two years now. I know the care she gives our customers is above average because of the care she has given me and her mother through this trial. Her fortitude is amazing because she has done all of this while also caring for her husband, Richard, as he waited for his second liver transplant. I want to recognize Richard's first liver donor, Matthew McCord, and thank his family for the eight-plus extra years we've had to love Richard thus far, and say that we are grateful for Richard's second donor and we are praying for his family. If it is God's will, we will one day know and love this family as well as we know and love Matthew's family. Each day is a cherished gift. Thank you.

Jim Norman, Julie's husband, has spent many nights alone since Julie began traveling with me and her mother to help me on the Get Motivated Seminar platforms and at other corporate events. I can't thank Jim enough for feeding Julie's three horses, three dogs, three cats, and one turtle, as well as watering her Elm Creek Memorial Garden when we are on the road. I know his sacrifice is no small thing, and I appreciate his attitude of love and support.

Chachis and Alexandra Ziglar, Tom's wife and daughter, have been patient and understanding about all the extra time Tom has spent and is still spending helping me and his mother since my fall. Tom has also assisted me personally by taking me to the gym five days a week to work out with a personal trainer. He, Cindy, and Julie all take turns going to doctors with me and the Redhead; and now when they say they are afraid we might forget to tell them what the doctor said, I know they have a legitimate concern!

Katherine Witmeyer Lemons, my granddaughter who does an incredible job as operations manager at our company, kept things going at the office when Tom, Cindy, and Julie were all out tending to me and the Redhead. We literally could not have covered all the bases without her. I'm keeping an eye on that one. . . . I do believe she's in line for Tom's position!

Jay Hellwig is someone who brings joy and light into our midst. Jay has driven me to my appointments and to catch innumerable airline flights through the years, but his activities this past year included verbally interviewing me for this book as we drove from one appointment to another. Julie would give him a list of questions, he'd record our conversations, Laurie Magers would transcribe the tapes, and Julie would figure out how to use my answers in *Embrace the Struggle*. It is really amazing how teamwork works, and I'm grateful Jay is on my team! His constant prayers with and for me warm my heart.

Each and every employee of Ziglar, Inc., deserves a round of applause. All have carried more than their own weight these past few years and have lived up to what I teach about being a team player. At my time of need they were there for me, the Redhead, and the rest of our family. None of us had to be concerned about what was happening at the office during those weeks and months after my accident. We knew everyone was taking care of everything. There was, and still is, great peace in that knowledge. I thank each of them for that priceless gift.

No acknowledgment of mine would be complete without mentioning how thankful I am to Tamara and Peter Lowe of the Get Motivated Seminars. First, to Tamara for allowing me to share some of her story in this book; and second, to Peter for coming up with the idea to interview me onstage after my fall. The gift of still being able to share my years of experience with audiences across this great nation of ours is a blessing to me and, I pray, to others. Our friendship and business relationship spans more than two decades, and I'm grateful for every one of those days!

This book would not exist without the generous, selfless sharing of life stories by people who have personally faced and some who still face their struggles. Each name that follows represents someone who took the time to tell us their story either in person or in writing, and Julie and I both want to express our deepest appreciation to them for being transparent and willing to share so that others might be helped. Thank you: Megan Mellquist; longtime friend Paula Reed; best friend Bernie Lofchick; Art Anderson; my granddaughter Elizabeth Witmeyer; Logan, Michael, and Tyra Shannon; my son-in-law Richard Oates; my friends Michael Godwin, Dave Ramsey, and Gail McWilliams.

To Kristi Brown, Deborah, John Plank, Pam, Preston Dixon, Mike Powers, Pansy Kennedy, Randy Welch, Charles Keith Hawkes and his wife Sandy, Sharon and William Cothron, Linda and Gary Van Buren, Kristena Smith-Rivera, Cheryl Bierley (for sharing the story of her father, Owen Arnold), my oldest granddaughter DeDe Galindo, longtime friend Bill Blain, Gaither Family Fest friend Marilyn Faulkner, Laura Johnson (Reichert), Jodie Butler, Bill McArthur, and our best domino buddy, Laurel Marshall: thanks to you all!

Lastly, I wouldn't have anyone to thank if it weren't for our wonderful book agents, Sealy and Matt Yates of Yates & Yates, putting us in touch with Howard Books, a division of Simon & Schuster! Thank you for believing in this book and helping us get it into the hands of those who are in the midst of embracing their struggles. We are grateful to Denny Boultinghouse, our editor at Howard Books, for all of the creative thought and work that has gone into making *Embrace the Struggle* the best it can possibly be. His attitude of helpfulness and willingness has made him a pleasure to work with. We also want to thank his assistant, Susan Wilson, and mention what a great time we had when Howard Books sent Chrys Howard and Michelle Tripp to take pictures for the cover of the book when we spoke at a Get Motivated Seminar in Austin, Texas. We've never had so much fun on a photo shoot! When it was over, we knew God had orchestrated the union of Howard Books and Ziglar, Inc., because the fit is perfect!

And I thank God, above all others, for allowing me to continue doing what I love to do.

Zig Ziglar

Julie Ziglar Norman

I want to thank Jesus Christ for being my Lord and Savior, my King, my heavenly Father, and my Bridegroom. I thank Him for bringing me out of the ashes of despair, for forgiving me and making me His. I desire to praise, worship, and serve Him all of my days.

My kind and generous husband, James (Jim) Curtis Norman, is the individual I most want to thank for his part in helping me both during the writing of this book and whenever I am on the road with Dad. Jim encourages me to keep doing what I'm doing, even though I can see that the cost to him is high. We both are blessed to work from home, but when one of us has to go out of town it can get lonely in a hurry. I also want to thank him for being the kind of husband every woman wants. He freely gives me his love and his attention, and he truly desires what is best for me. He somehow deals with my being entirely too literal and keeps on smiling through it all. I love you, honey!

My parents have always loved me and I've always known that I am loved. I am blessed to travel with them when Dad and I speak, and I cherish our time together on the road. I thank God for the relationship I have with both of them. Working with Dad has led me down a path I could not have imagined, and I can't wait to see what is next. Seeing Mom come alongside Dad is an example of deep, committed love that I hope and pray I can emulate in my own marriage. I am grateful to be their child.

My children have survived more book deadlines than children ought to have to survive! They have foraged for food while I slaved away all hours of the night and day. They are grown now, but they still feel the difference in my availability when book deadlines loom large, as do my precious grandchildren. I thank my son, James (Jim) E. Norman, and my daughters, DeDe Galindo, Jenni Haecker, and Amey Fair, for being patient and understanding all these years. Dad and I have used stories about them in many of Dad's books, so I want to thank them for that and for making me a grandmother twelve times over. Children are a blessing from the Lord, and I am so proud of mine!

My brother, Tom Ziglar, and sister, Cindy Oates, are anchors of love that represent security and support for me. Only they fully know what it is like to have both of our parents on hospital gurneys at the same time. I love how close we are and that all three of us feel equally responsible for helping our parents in any way that is needed. I cannot imagine not having their love and support—and they are my biggest cheerleaders, as Dad would say. I thank them both.

I want to thank Tutti Proffit Bowles for a literal lifetime of best friendship. We have kept each other's secrets so long, neither one of us can remember them! Paula Reed is and has always been a tremendous source of encouragement and unconditional love and acceptance. Steve Levey is the best guy friend ever, and this book has caused a few missed visits. My Alvord girlfriend Kay Brooks has been patient, encouraging, and supportive regardless of the amount of time that passes between our visits. And what would a girl do without her saddle pals? These ladies have ridden their horses with me; and the trails we've traveled have often mimicked our lives—unpredictable and sometimes more exciting than we bargained for. We have shared our victories and failures, our grief and our joys. And our outings have given me much-needed, refreshing breaks. Thank you, Lynn Cacy; Beth Manuel, who taught me how to be a good saddle pal in the first place; Diane Dean, whose beloved Candy's Man brought us together; Leslie Francis; Emmy Mobley; Hollie Carron; Marilyn Gilbert; Jayne O'Reilly; Linda Delwood; Dona Fioretti; Amber Roberts; Becky Zimmerman; Connie Burgdorf; Dona Ivy; Mary LaCoste; and my special friend and mentor in and out of the saddle, Lynne Tracy.

I doubt seriously that I would have agreed to speak on stage with Dad had it not been for the biblical instruction that my pastor Gene Smith gave me from the pulpit and in personal conversations over the past decade. I want to thank him for teaching me what it is to be obedient to God. He taught me that God would put before me what He intended for me to do but that I had to be available, willing, and obedient to be of any use to Him. Gene's wife, Janice, has been an example of living for God. She showed me what it means to be a truly surrendered bondservant of the Lord. When I surrendered my WHOLE life to God in Columbus, Ohio, on November 13, 2007, confessed that my life was not my own, and said, "Here I am Lord. Send me!" I knew that God had used Gene and Janice to prepare me for that very moment. I thank God for putting them in my life.

I've saved for last my dear friend and confidante, the person I work most closely with, and the one who does more than anyone to help me look good. I know I would not be in this position if she had not been behind me these past sixteen years. Thank you, thank you, thank you, Laurie Magers! When I started editing for Dad I didn't have any practical experience and Laurie took care of me. Over the years we've laughed and cried, wondered aloud, been each other's memories, prayed and stayed up late, gotten up early and seen twenty-six book deadlines come and go. I treasure her friendship and her incredible level of competence. Laurie is my rock, and I am grateful beyond words to have her in my life.

Julie Ziglar Norman

Printed in the United States
By Bookmasters